# YOUR SOUL'S WHISPERS

## A Journey of Awakening

Hannelore

Book One in the

*Your Soul's Whispers Trilogy*

To Dr. Bill -
Thank you for being
such an incredible gift
of light to us all.

Illustrations by Visionary Artist

Francene Hart

Blessings
Hannelore ♡

ISBN: 978-1-9991693-2-9

Publisher: Peace by Peace Publishing

Address: Burnaby, British Columbia, Canada

Email: Hannelore@Hannelore.ca

Website: www.Hannelore.ca

# Contents

# Notes About Quotes

Numerous quotes are included throughout the *Your Soul's Whispers Trilogy*. Original Hannelore quotes are indicated by her signature spiral.

**On our shared journey of awakening,**
**to truly "see" One another,**
**we must look past One another's humanness**
**so that we may wholeheartedly embrace**
**One another's divineness.**

Many of Hannelore's favorite quotes by others are incased within textboxes and are occasionally decorated with a butterfly.

**"Go inside and listen to your body, because your body will never lie to you. Your mind will play tricks, but the way you feel in your heart, in your guts, is the truth."**

**~ Miguel Ruiz**

**"If I go into the place in myself that is love, and you go into the place in yourself that is love, we are together in love. Then you and I are truly in love, the state of being love. That's the entrance to Oneness."**

**~ Ram Dass**

## In Praise of *Your Soul's Whispers*

"Hannelore's books are like an exquisite tapestry—carefully woven into each paragraph is a beautiful timeless message that miraculously resurrects the soul. Look to 'see' the deeper meaning while appreciating her chronicles."

**~ Charles Patterson, author of *Out of the Blue-Into the Now* and developer of *Synchronetix* (premiering summer 2020).**

"Describing Hannelore's book, *Your Soul's Whispers,* is like expressing a smile.

I met Hannelore years ago at one of her Communing with Dolphins retreats in Hawaii. It was life-changing for me. She is gentle and kind, a remarkable teacher, sparks laughter, and is respectful of an individual's journey. This comes through in her book which is brimming with wisdom. Easy to understand and thought-provoking, her book takes you on a magical inner and outer journey. The many stories in the book, invite awe and wonder as they ignite your imagination.

Without a doubt, this book will have a positive impact on your life as it already has on mine."

**~ Gloria Jean. Creator of Gloria Jean's Coffee and author of *Journey of Prayer* and *The Journey of Gloria Jean.***

"Through exquisite storytelling and profound understanding, Hannelore offers adventures into self-discovery and universal wisdom. Her words gently expand our vision of how consciousness evolves and opens heart and mind to the oneness we share."

**~ Francene Hart, author and visionary artist.**

"From the moment I started reading *Your Souls Whispers,* I literally could not put it down.

The stories resonated with my entire being and were incredibly touching. Sometimes, I cried when I was supposed to laugh, and maybe vice versa.

Thanks to the insights, inspiration and healing I received by reading this book, I know that my purpose is to use my spiritual gifts to help others. I look forward to reading the next remarkable book in the trilogy."

**~ Susan Buchik, author.**

"By sharing her intimate experiences, Hannelore helps us to make sense of our inner and outer worlds. With tremendous wisdom and coming from a place of love, Hannelore gives the reader practical tools to begin one's own spiritual journey. A must read for anyone wondering, 'Who am I?' or 'What is my purpose in life?'"

**~ Serena Thiel, designer and entrepreneur.**

"I loved reading *Your Soul's Whispers!*

Throughout the book, Hannelore shares personal stories and relatable experiences to lovingly inspire and gently guide others toward a deeper awakening and clearer understanding of *self*.

I am grateful and pleased to recommend this book. I can't wait for the next one!"

**~ Lynda Stevenson (Dear Auntie),**
**author/creator *Owner's Manual* app.**

"I really enjoyed working through Hannelore's amazing book. I love that she included so many relatable stories, many of which created *aha* moments for me. Others reminded me of things I learned during my spiritual awakening process and had forgotten.

Every time I felt the need to read the next chapter, I either learned something new, or was reminded of exactly what I needed to know in that moment to help me with whatever had shown up in my life.

Thank you so much for creating this trilogy. I know it will assist everyone whose hands it ends up in!"

**~ Cindy Thomas, LPN, Reiki master and Vega technician.**

"Hannelore is a most compassionate, heart-centered and gifted writer. These gifts shine through within each page. Reading this thought-provoking book feels like chatting with a dear friend over tea. She shares her personal experiences so deeply, and leaves the reader with many practical tools to assist them along their journey.

The rich content in *Your Soul's Whispers* is a life changer even if only half of the information is acted upon. I'm excitedly anticipating the next book!"

**~ Dianna Watson, author & facilitator.**

"Hannelore has a remarkable gift of giving one a gentle push to move on to the next level of their awareness and to let go of what no longer serves them.

There is something in this book for everyone no matter where you are on your path of awakening. It is easy to follow, and is a *great reminder for those of us who have been on the path for some time.*

I love that the pages are not filled with psychic babble, but are brimming with believable, gently sweet and thought-provoking stories that deeply touched me.

Reading this book is like sitting on your couch having a cup of tea with Hannelore. Thank you for opening my heart, and for reminding me it is okay to cry and to remember to laugh."

**~ Rachel Cuyler, intuitive counselor.**

"What a wonderful collection of stories and examples of awakening to Spirit and to one's self! Hannelore provides easy to follow steps and practical tools to assist you on your journey and help you connect to the whisper of your own soul. Her knowledge and authenticity leap from the pages as she shares her teachings.

Thanks, Hannelore. *Your Soul's Whispers: A Journey of Awakening* is a must read. I am looking forward to reading your next book."

**~ Gayle Evanik, energy practitioner.**

"We are all sojourners, each of us navigating fears and distractions as we search for meaning, for purpose, for love.

Reading *YOUR SOUL'S WHISPERS: A Journey of Awakening* reminded me that the answers I seek are readily accessible when I listen to the inner voice of my intuition and accept the guidance of synchronous happenings.

The *awakening processes* in the book reconnected me with the truths of my heart and the empowering energies of intention, gratitude and trust.

Hannelore's personal and poignant stories reaffirmed my knowing that we are beloved brothers and sisters of a common parent—the All That Is.

No matter where you are on your journey inward and homeward, I highly recommend this delightful and insightful compilation of divine wisdom."

**~ Joy Ross, author, editor & publisher.**

# Dedication

**I dedicate this book and the entire *Your Soul's Whispers Trilogy* to my beloved mother, Barbara Thiel.** Mom, you were my confidant, my light, my teacher...my best friend. You taught me pure unconditional love and inspired me to be all that I am. I loved the "me" that you saw. You helped me find the courage to transcend the many challenges in my life, and although your light now shines from the other side, it is your voice I continue to hear encouraging me to write.

**I also dedicate this book and the *Your Soul's Whispers Trilogy* to my brilliant sister, Serena.** You are my best friend and the earth angel God remembered to send. We are there for one another in the good times and bad, openly sharing our joys, tears and laughter. I am grateful that you always go above and beyond in your dedication and support of my teaching and writing journeys, willingly contributing your many creative talents. Serena, thank you for always inspiring me to reach for the stars.

**This book and the trilogy would not have been possible without my dear teacher, Sharon.** Sharon, I miss you dearly. I know you continue to guide me from the other side. You were the one who showed me the missing piece in my life, opening my eyes and the door to my spiritual journey. You continue to be my mentor. We had many insightful experiences, one of which proved you were my ultimate and most profound teacher. I am eternally grateful we had one last magical adventure together playing with our dolphin friends.

# Thank You!

**I thank my father whose twinkling eyes made me sparkle.** To this day, you are my loving guide from beyond the veil. I love you Dad.

**To the rest of my family**, especially my son, Sean, his wife, Val, and their three precious children, Taegan, Riley and Isla, who call me Nana. To my daughter, Kyra, who reminds me I have more to learn. To my brother, Ralph, and his wife, Elaine, who offered me their lovely home in Arizona as a retreat where I could finally complete this trilogy.

To my nieces, nephews, aunts, uncles, cousins, and many very dear and supportive friends—without you, life would not shine as brightly.

**A special thank you to my brilliant editor and proofreaders.** I am deeply moved and incredibly grateful for your support, dedication and patience. Your hours of work and great catches helped to ensure that this book is the best it can be.

**A special thank you to my beloved friend and muse Francene Hart** for allowing me to grace the pages of this book with her wonderful sacred geometry artwork. Widely sought after by collectors around the globe, Francene's paintings bridge the gap between this reality and the metaphysical world of healing, continuity and transformation. For more information about Francene, her creations and her workshops, visit https://francenehart.com.

**From the bottom of my heart, I appreciate and thank you all.**

# Message from Hannelore

**There is something tugging at your heart,**
**a whisper from your soul that says...**
***"Live your purpose before it's too late. You are here for much greater, grander things than this!"***

## YOUR SOUL'S WHISPERS TRILOGY

Thank you for reading the first edition in the long-anticipated *Your Soul's Whispers Trilogy.* Together, we will awaken from this world of illusion and embark on a *journey of awakening*.

I consider myself to be an inspirational and motivational storyteller. I'm grateful for this opportunity to share my personal experiences of growth, some painful and others exhilarating. You may even recognize yourself within these pages.

My writings and teachings come from my heart and my truth. This does not mean that my experiences and insights are the only way or the absolute right way to a journey of awakening. I invite and encourage you, as the reader, to trust what feels right and resonates with you and to set aside what does not.

Rather than being an in-depth study, each book in the trilogy is a sampling of many topics intended to inspire you to listen to the whispers of your soul.

**As we embark on this journey of awakening,
pause and listen to the whispers of your soul,
for you are connected to all intelligence in the universe.**

One of my greatest lessons was learning to surrender to love, not fear. For a long while, I resisted and challenged what the whispers of my inner voice had to share. In hindsight, I smile as I recognize that in my surrendering, the whisperings of my inner voice led me to my journey of awakening and to know that I always have the choice—to allow fear to get in my way...or to express love.

This book and the entire trilogy are intended to support you by offering information and processes for expanded mindfulness. The pages are filled with powerful thought-provoking stories, parables and practical techniques to help you fully comprehend your *inner* and *outer* worlds.

You will be gently guided to let go of and transform any fears relating to self-worth, abandonment and trust. You will also be presented with the opportunity to activate and unleash the "force" that is within. As this *awareness* is practiced and becomes part of your daily life, personally and professionally, it will magnify your infinite potential.

As you awaken from a world of illusion, you will know your purpose and recognize the brilliance of your being.

***Together, we can be the change we wish to see in the world.***

## On Spirituality

Throughout the *Your Soul's Whispers Trilogy*, I interchangeably use the words God, Spirit, Creator, Source, the All That Is, and Universal Life Force Energy to refer to an energy "force" that exists within all living things. Please feel free to replace my references with whatever title resonates with you.

In our desire to stay connected to a belief, we accept religious teachings that connect with the state of wholeness and understanding that our level of consciousness accepts. As a student of comparative religions, I discovered numerous wonderful and profound beliefs with many organizations espousing a particular doctrine as being the one true path. I also noted that each had a common thread—a belief in one divine being.

I believe we are all One. However, there are infinite ways to approach "God," and I honor the choice of the individual and respect each one's faith.

The *Your Soul's Whispers Trilogy* explores and encourages mindful awareness. It is not about religion, for that is a powerful and complex topic that I will not endeavor to address. Nor do I promote one path over another. Rather, as I consider myself as being *spiritual*, my writings reflect my chosen path, my life's purpose.

## On Metaphysics

The information in the *Your Soul's Whispers Trilogy* and the content of my transformational courses and experiential retreats all touch on the many aspects of the metaphysical.

Before we tap into the realm of metaphysics, let's look at the word itself.

> *Meta* means about the thing itself, being self-aware, and looking at things from a higher perspective.
>
> *Physics* is a branch of science that delves into the properties of matter, nature and energy.
>
> *Metaphysics* is a branch of philosophy that explores the first cause, the nature and origin of existence.

When one delves into metaphysics, it may be to explore the aspects of psychology, mysticism, parapsychology, ESP, psychic phenomena, philosophy, psychotherapy, religion, meditation, yoga, self-help and improvement, the power of positive thinking, life force energy, life after death, reincarnation, and/or spirituality, to name just a few.

All metaphysical pursuits involve the search for truth, purpose, meaning in life, and the desire to make our world a better place.

For those who approach life from an intellectual, practical or logical way of thinking, stepping into the world of metaphysics evokes a wonderful stretch of the imagination.

**"The intellect has little to do on the road to discovery. There comes a leap in consciousness, call it intuition or what you will, and the solution comes to you and you don't know how or why."**

**~ Albert Einstein**

I offer information about metaphysics as a segue to the many processes included in this edition of the *Your Soul's Whispers Trilogy*. These mindfulness exercises are not the only way to an enlightened and purposeful life journey, nor are they meant to downplay the importance of one-on-one counseling for those in the process of healing.

**I invite you to stretch your imagination.**

**Everything is INTENTION.**

**May the wisdom I share help illuminate your way.**

# Prologue: How my Spiritual Journey Began

## Story: What a Difference a Day Makes

It was 6 a.m. on a perfect and beautiful morning. I proudly had my many pledges with me and was on my way to meet a friend. We were both going on a walk for MS (multiple sclerosis). My two dalmatians were safely snuggled in the back seat, and my *Deep Breakfast* CD filled the car with celestial music. My life seemed great. My heart was filled with joy and gratitude.

Then WHAM!!!

Seemingly out of nowhere, a truck ran a red light and smashed into the driver's side of my car. Time slowed as my car spun several times, and hundreds of small fragments of glass showered the front seat. The sound of metal being crunched replaced the song on my CD. Then all was black as I lost consciousness.

When I came to, the police and ambulance were already on the scene. Off in the distance, I could hear myself repeating, "I am sure it was a green light. I am sure it was a green light."

As I slowly came back into my body, I heard a police officer call for someone to pick up my dogs. I adamantly said, "No!" When the attendants placed me on a gurney and into the ambulance, I insisted we drive to the parking lot where my friend was waiting for me. As soon as I knew she was going to take care of my dogs, I relaxed and went into shock.

I had a massive head injury that impaired the cognitive functioning of the left side of my brain. I lost a great deal of my memory and had to relearn to speak. It took tremendous effort to say each word.

***Why did this happen?*** As I reflected on my life prior to the accident, the answer as to why it had happened gradually came to me. I did not have the courage to let go of a life path that no longer served me. I was not living my intended purpose.

## My Life Prior to the Car Accident

I thought that I was living my dream.

In my twenties, I was passionate about the film industry. I had a very successful career as a professional actress and model. Trust, perseverance, listening to my inner voice, and applying intuitive strategies played a key role in that success.

As models are encouraged to do, I created a portfolio filled with images that displayed my diversity. I then showed it to numerous ad agencies, photographers and photo studios. This process is called "go sees."

I didn't realize it at the time, but throughout my modelling career, my intuition was in full force. Whenever I perused a list of names, I intuitively knew who the key players and best photographers were. Knowing it would propel my career forward, I negotiated with several photographers, offering my time and modelling expertise so that they could *test* new looks. It was a win-win situation.

As my portfolio grew, I repeatedly revisited the "key" people on my go-see list. Within two years, I experienced a very successful career as a professional actress and model. I appeared in over one hundred television commercials, on the cover of many magazines, in catalogues, on billboards, in newspapers, on television shows, and had several small parts in movies.

**But life was also filled with challenges.**

I put my career on hold to salvage my marriage and spend time with my two children. After several years, a failed marriage, and now a single parent, I returned to the film industry, reactivated my career, and studied marketing.

Once I obtained a degree in marketing, I created and was the CEO of what became a successful marketing company in the film industry. I exclusively represented several large production companies and was an agent for over fifty high-profile directors of commercials. I also contracted with a prominent music production company and a few animation companies.

Travelling was a big part of my business as my clients were the creative teams of the major advertising agencies in sixteen cities throughout Canada and the United States.

**I am so very grateful for my intuitive internal antenna.**

As a marketing director, one must be keenly aware of who, when, where, and how to create and implement effective strategies.

Because I paid attention to my intuition, developing these strategies was easy for me.

I enjoyed a glamorous and lucrative lifestyle. I worked with many high-profile celebrities and was at the top of my field doing what I loved.

Intellectually, I thought I was living my passion; however, I couldn't shake the feeling or sense that something was missing in my life. ***But what was that something?***

I noticed this more and more as the years went by. Often, I asked myself two questions:

**"If I was to die today, what have I contributed to our planet?"**

**"What am I meant to do?"**

I knew I wanted a change in my life, but I did not know what to change. I found that the more I continued doing what I no longer loved to do, the unhappier I felt. I became increasingly negative and began to hugely dislike what I previously enjoyed.

**Have you ever had the feeling or sense inside of you that something was missing, something not complete?**

**If you have, the next story is for you.**

## Story: Synchronicities Were Set in Motion

***When the student is ready, the teacher will arrive.***

After a lengthy business trip, I often treated myself to a few days in a quiet and delightful bed-and-breakfast cottage overlooking a small lake. While there, I relaxed and meditated.

During one of my mini-retreats, I felt a noticeable ache in my heart, a deep yearning. Not knowing what the yearning was, I asked that I *see*, *feel* or *hear* my angels and guides. Tears streaming down my cheeks, **I asked God, "What am I meant to do? Why do I feel like something urgent is missing?"**

After a long while, it seemed as though I would not get a response. Feeling depleted, I surrendered. **It was then that I heard a gentle whisper, "Go for a walk."**

As it was nearby, I decided to walk to one of my favorite little seaside towns. I'd visited the town's numerous quaint little shops many times before. This time, I noticed a cobblestone-paved street leading into a narrow alley, and was surprised that I had never noticed it before. **Once again, I heard a whisper, "Go explore."**

While entering one store, I noticed a sign by the door that read:

**Books - Crystals**
**Cards - Gifts**
**Readings**

Thinking that it might be a little quirky but would also be fun and interesting, I decided to go in and have a reading. Maybe a psychic could help me discover what was missing in my life.

Once inside, the clerk told me that the person who owned the store and did the readings was not in and wasn't expected back for a few days. She also asked if I would be interested in a phone reading. I thought it was a strange idea, so I said, "No, thanks. I'll just have a look around." (As a side note, I have now done many hundreds of phone readings.)

As fate would have it, a few seconds later, the owner walked into the store. Approaching me, she said, "I'm Sharon. I understand you are interested in a reading."

I'd never had a reading before, and suddenly wondered if I really wanted one. Regardless, I said, "Yes."

Sharon gazed deeply into my eyes, and asked, "When?"

Caught in her gaze, I replied, "Now."

### What Happened Next Changed My Life

My reading was incredible and profound. In response to the information Sharon shared, I felt tremendous body rushes, got goose bumps, and experienced a wide range of emotions. The sensations were intense and surreal. I kept wondering whether my chair was emitting sporadic electrical charges. (I later learned that body rushes are one's *higher self* acknowledging a truth.)

During the reading, a great aunt who'd crossed over had a message for me, as did a dear old departed dog. Sharon also offered numerous amazing insights about me and my life. At the end of the reading, I asked, "Do you teach how to do this?"

### My Spiritual Journey Began

A whole new chapter opened in my life. In addition to studying advanced clairvoyant training with Sharon, I embarked on a quest for knowledge, learning whatever I could find that had to do with spirituality.

I went on what I refer to as a *feeding frenzy*. I studied and became a Reiki master, attended medicine and mystery schools, studied qi gong, psychosomatic therapy, alchemical hypnotherapy, shamanism, kundalini breath and eye techniques, and attended countless other classes and seminars.

One of my courses was with The New Seminary. Affiliated with the University of New York, teachings were focused on the study of comparative religions and the dimensions of psychology. A few years later, I was ordained as an interfaith minister at the Cathedral of St. John the Divine located in New York City.

Two notable creeds of an interfaith minister are:

**"Not instead of, but in addition to"**
and **"We are all One."**

When I and my fellow students were ordained as interfaith ministers, we were asked to offer a personal vow and commitment to God. Below is mine.

**Divine Spirit, Beloved Mother/Father God,**
**I give myself to You as an open channel**
**in total love and commitment.**
**That I may be an instrument of peace, love and inspiration.**
**That my voice is Your voice and my actions Your actions.**
**That I touch in some way, the souls of this planet**
**on their journey of awakening to their light.**
**May I become as one with Your light,**
**and with Your grace,**
**as I touch all those that cross my path.**
***So Be It and So It Is***

### Seeing What Was Not There

I studied for several years with my new teacher, Sharon. I became her protégé, and she, my best friend and mentor.

Many months after we met, Sharon said, "I have always meant to ask you this. Do you remember the day you came into my store?"

"Of course," I replied.

She asked, "How did you know that I did readings?"

I said, "It was on the sign in front of your store."

What Sharon then said will remain with me always: "Yes, I know the sign. But I don't advertise readings, honey."

***Readings* was never on that sign!**

Destiny led me to my spiritual journey by opening a part of me that was dormant. I have since learned that we will see what we are meant to see, and when we are ready, the teacher will be there.

### I Found My Missing ~~Piece~~ Peace

Having found my missing *peace*, I knew that my true purpose was to pursue my spiritual path and to be of service to others. With my awakening in mind, I began downsizing my company. As it would mean letting go of a substantial income and financial security, I didn't have the courage to release my business completely.

Disillusioned with the film industry, it no longer inspired me, no longer brought me joy. Yet, the more I focused on my spiritual path, the more my film business kept pulling me back.

I soon discovered that when you are meant to be doing something else with your life and you don't have the courage to let go and move forward, what happens is that you are eventually hit over the head, or you lose your footing and twist an ankle, or something drastic happens; in my case, it was a car accident.

Because I didn't have the courage to let go of a career that had completed its meaningful time with me, and had yet to pursue my universe-intended purpose wholeheartedly, Spirit stepped in and threw a truck in my path.

## Back to the Beginning of My Story

Following the car accident, I lost my confidence. Suffering from memory loss, remembering the detailed steps I needed to do to promote my film company was extremely challenging. As a result, I cancelled many meetings and gradually let go of all but one contract.

In time, I was able to regain my speech and became a professional speaker. Even though I still experience challenges with my memory, I can share my spiritual knowledge clearly. The reason—I speak from my heart, not my head.

## More Synchronicities Put into Place

After several months, my last remaining contract was not renewed. A day later, a power surge caused my computer to crash. My business records were lost; yet, my spiritual files were magically backed up. I know I didn't back up my files as I didn't know how to do so.

During the same power surge, my business answering machine was fried. Interestingly, the device I used for my personal and spiritual classes was unharmed and still worked.

**I finally said, "Okay, God. I get it."**

I continued developing my spiritual practice, and centered my focus on creating classes, developing seminars, and one-on-one counselling. I love to teach through my personal experiences—to share what brought me joy and made a huge difference in my life.

I've worked with many individuals who also felt lost. Taking each one gently and firmly through the process of stepping into their fear and through their pain, I've witnessed astounding courage as each one journeyed into his/her light and magnificence. To witness people's lives transform is my greatest joy. I feel blessed to have God use me as an instrument of peace in this way.

# CH 1: Magnificent Brilliance Within

**"The heart is a temple wherein all truth resides."**

**~ George Burns**

All that you seek—the peace, love and answers—are within you, always were and always will be. As you come to fully comprehend your inner and outer worlds, you will awaken from this world of illusion. You will embrace the *truth* of who you are and know your intended path, for it is then that you will embrace the brilliance of your being.

The following insight is from Jesus's secret teachings in the **Gospel of Thomas**.

**"If you bring forth what is within you,**
**what you bring forth will save you.**
**If you do not bring forth what is within,**
**what you do not bring forth will destroy you."**

**"The best way to find yourself
is to lose yourself in the service of others."**

**~ Gandhi**

It is never too late! As long as you still have breath, you can bring forth and give life to what is within you. It is when you bury the potential within that you bury your joy and diminish your light.

## AWAKENING PROCESS

***Open to the Whispers of Your Soul***

If you are unclear as to the nature of the brilliance within you, practice being open to receiving and hearing the whispers of your soul. Whispers are inherent in your intuition, unexpected and/or sudden inspirations, and in what you love to do. You may have felt but not fully recognized glimpses of your soul's awakening in your heart. Going forward, embrace these whispers and be willing to take risks so that you may set yourself free.

I invite you to reflect on the poem titled "Risks" on the next page.

As writing down your thoughts, feelings and insights will enhance your ever-evolving inner knowings—*Your Soul's Whispers*—I also invite you to keep a journal of your awakenings as you venture through the processes in this book.

## RISKS

*"To laugh is to risk appearing the fool.*
*To weep is to risk appearing sentimental.*
*To reach out for another is to risk involvement.*
*To expose feelings is to risk exposing your true self.*
*To place your ideas, your dreams before*
*a crowd is to risk their loss.*
*To love is to risk not being loved in return,*
*To live is to risk dying.*
*To hope is to risk despair.*
*To try is to risk failure.*
*But risks must be taken, because the greatest*
*hazard in life is to risk nothing.*
*The person who risks nothing, does nothing,*
*has nothing and is nothing.*
*They may avoid suffering and sorrow but*
*they cannot learn, feel, change, grow, love or live.*
*Chained by their certitudes, they are a slave,*
*For they have forfeited their freedom.*
*Only the person who risks is truly free."*

~ **Anonymous**

**"Sometimes a person needs a story more than food to stay alive."**

**~ Barry Lopez**

## Story: My Writing Journey

My writing journey has been a long and challenging one. I started in the late nineties, feeling inspired and enthusiastic and with several book ideas. As the years passed, I wrote a great deal but found precious little time to compile my material into book format. My schedule was jam-packed with teaching classes, counseling, and creating programs, seminars and retreats.

I recognized the importance of creating a space to write that sparked inspiration, and at the same time, nurtured my body, mind and spirit. Like it is for almost everyone, being in nature nourishes my being, and what better space than camping on a sandy beach at a bay the dolphins regularly frequent.

For several years, just prior to facilitating my *Communing with Dolphins* retreats in Hawaii, I camped at a favorite bay and spent my early mornings swimming with my dolphin friends. Being among these playful creatures filled me with joy and inspiring images. The rest of my days were spent transcribing these heartfelt conceptualizations and messages into my writings.

At long last, in 2009, I rented a small cottage in Hawaii and dedicated several months to focusing entirely on completing my book. I felt a huge sense of accomplishment. I finally had my completed book on my laptop! I deleted my recorded talks and threw away the many handwritten notes now all neatly transcribed. As a precaution, I backed everything onto a separate portable hard drive.

Upon my return home to Vancouver, British Columbia, the first thing I planned to do was upload my book onto my main computer. Instead, I left everything on the dining room table and invited my daughter out for a celebratory lunch.

When we arrived back at the house, the doors were wide open. Noticing that my flat screen TV was missing, I immediately glanced toward the dining room table. My laptop and portable hard drive were gone, and my book along with them. My heart sank. Many other items were also missing, but what devastated me most was losing my book. All that work! I questioned whether I was even meant to write. I felt deflated.

> **"If you really believe in what you're doing, work hard, take nothing personally and if something blocks one route, find another. Never give up."**
>
> **~ Laurie Notaro**

It took a while, but once I was over the shock, something deep inside urged me to keep writing. My inner voice insisted, **"Don't give up! You still have it all inside you!"**

**"Most of us have two lives.**
**The life we live and the unlived life within us.**
**Between the two stands resistance."**
**~ Steven Pressfield**

I channeled the energy of disillusionment and disappointment into planting and nurturing my backyard garden. Blessed with a warm and sunny spring and summer, I surrounded my outdoor gazebo with colorful flowering hanging baskets. This was my secret garden and sanctuary where I began rewriting my book.

I was once again filled with joy as I became the guardian of two sets of nesting birds that had chosen my flower baskets to bring new life into the world. As I watched them tend their eggs, I too felt I was tending to the new birth of my creation.

While in this place of joy, I discovered I preferred the way the book was unfolding. New ideas presented themselves as I was inspired to continue. It seemed as though I was guided by an invisible force.

**The journey of one's life is filled with**
**joys and with sorrow.**
**Maintaining a positive perspective can prove challenging**.

The fall, winter and early spring were filled with distractions as I promoted and facilitated retreats, spoke at functions, and taught classes. After my 2011 Dolphin retreats in Hawaii, I put all my belongings into storage, rented a remote cottage and focused my attention entirely on writing and the completion of my book.

My mother was my muse. I started each day by reading to her over the phone what I'd written the previous day. There were times after reading a passage that there was silence at the other end of the phone. "Mom, are you there?" I'd ask. At which she would respond with a quivering voice, "That was so beautiful."

Grateful for her inspiration, my intention was to dedicate my book to her and launch it on Mother's Day, May of 2012. My beloved mother passed unexpectedly on October 18, 2011.

**"Recognize that on certain days the greatest grace is that the day is over, and you get to close your eyes."**

**~ Mary Anne Radmacher**

I fell into a deep depression, and my book was set aside as my writing came to a screeching halt. A huge part of my soul went with my mother. Disconnected, lost and consumed with melancholy, what is often referred to as the "the dark night of the soul" set in.

I was and remain soothed by **Kahlil Gibran's** comforting words in ***The Prophet***.

**"Your joy is your sorrow unmasked.**
**And the selfsame well from which your laughter rises**
**was oftentimes filled with your tears;**
**together they come**
**and when one sits alone with you at your board,**
**remember that the other is asleep upon your bed."**

I trusted my joy was simply resting. Yet, every time I ventured to pull myself up, I was met with more sorrow as nine friends and family passed within a year. Never before had I experienced such darkness and sorrow. My light diminished and a part of my soul split off.

**"Life is not about waiting for the storm to pass ...**
**it's about learning how to dance in the rain."**
**~ Vivian Green**

I facilitated a few workshops and accepted some speaking engagements. During this time, through remarkable synchronicities and messages of encouragement from those who had passed, I gradually began to "dance in the rain" as a new book was born: ***The Other side of the Window ~ Communing's from Beyond the Veil.***

Writing this book helped my heart heal. (*The Other Side of the Window* is gracefully waiting its turn to be published.)

In addition to seeking outside help to heal my emotional pain, with great perseverance, I called upon my teachings. I spent many hours taking myself through various processes using the tools and techniques I often shared with others.

I could never have imagined it would take me six years to once again pick up my book. The original title was "Ignite Your Sixth Sense, the Power of Your Intuition." However, as I went through my countless notes, they reminded me of the many "whispers" I'd received encouraging me to continue. The next whisper was the birthing of my new title: ***Your Soul's Whispers***.

In his book ***The War of Art,*** **Steven Pressfield** wrote about his struggles as a writer. I easily related to his experiences and insights on resistance.

> **"Resistance kills creativity, stifles our happiness and stunts the person that we are here to become. It repels, it distracts, and it derails us from the life we are meant to live."**

Resistance wore the mask of procrastination in my life. I would do almost anything to keep from writing as it felt overwhelming. I would garden, clean the house, do laundry, run errands or watch a movie. I found that sometimes I needed to *zone out* in order to *tune back in*.

**"Do not put off till tomorrow**
**what you can put off till the day after tomorrow."**
**~ Mark Twain**

**Son asks his father, *"What does procrastination mean?"***
**The father replies, *"I will tell you tomorrow."***

Renowned British author and playwright **Somerset Maugham** was asked if he wrote on a schedule or only when struck with inspiration. He responded, **"I write only when inspiration strikes. Fortunately, it strikes every morning at 9 o'clock sharp."**

For me, the hardest part was to sit down and start writing. Every time I walked away, it was like starting all over again, and the longer my absence, the harder it was to begin. Once in the flow, however, writing was easy and a joy.

Each time I reviewed what I'd written, I made changes, moving one section to another, and so on. I felt like a "master weaver" was guiding me as I continually weaved insights and information in and out of chapters.

> **Writing the *Your Soul's Whispers Trilogy* was an exciting and profound process of unraveling the truth of all that I know.**

Despite time gaps, misfortune and heartache, whenever I was ready, the universe provided the ideal location and circumstances for me to dedicate my full attention to writing. Each time I sat down to rewrite my book, I dedicated all of my time to writing, often putting in fifteen to eighteen hours per day.

My passion for writing, so that I may be of service to others, is why what was meant to be a single book transformed into the *Your Soul's Whispers Trilogy.* It's also why more books are in the offing.

Filled with overwhelming gratitude for the gift of being able to express in prose what the whispers of my soul had to share, I was showered with the heaven-inspired insights and inspirations that **Steven Pressfield** so eloquently wrote about in ***The War of Art.***

> **"Because when we sit down day after day and keep grinding, something mysterious starts to happen. A process is set into motion by which, inevitably and infallibly, heaven comes to our aid. Unseen forces enlist in our cause; serendipity reinforces our purpose."**
>
> **~ Steven Pressfield**

As I processed through yet another personal transformation, each page was often rewritten. Just as I would imagine a painter or potter continues to improve a work of art until the day comes when they let it go and *trust* that it is complete.

My process of transformation continued due to the intimate nature of the *Your Soul's Whispers Trilogy*. In allowing myself to be vulnerable in my sharing, if I had not *fully* embodied the lesson I was writing about, the universe presented me with the opportunity to relearn over and over again.

For example, the chapter on "Mirrors" in the second book in the trilogy was especially challenging and emotionally exhausting. It could not be completed until, out of integrity, I once again "got it." When writing the chapter on "Love vs Fear" in the third book, *fear* reared its head like a thief in the night as it robbed me of my much-needed rest, inviting me to once again embrace, transcend, and clear.

I live in the *trust* that all is in perfect timing. The book in 2009 would have been a completely different book, just as had I published the new version in 2012. With the ongoing transformations, I know there comes a time when I have to let go and trust in its completion.

**When we slow down and open ourselves**
**to hear the whispers within,**
**we can then realize we all have an angel, a muse who encourages us to create, to expand and to evolve.**

My mother continues to be my muse, my angel from the other side, as she keeps fulfilling her purpose to inspire. I realized that as much as I resisted and procrastinated returning to my writing, I allowed her messages of support to encourage me to continue.

I now rejoice in the birthing of the long-awaited books in the *Your Soul's Whispers Trilogy.*

May the journey and whispers of this book help bring awareness to your body, soul and spirit. As you keep your heart center awake, your soul will guide you to find a fearless and empowered place within you.

In trust, I invite you to join me as we move forward together in a shift of awakening.

**"Every blade of grass has an angel that bends over it**
**and whispers, 'Grow! Grow! Grow!'"**
**~ The Talmud**

# CH 2: Value Your Worth

All that you desire is waiting to unfold from within. Your life is precious, and it is a gift. You deserve all the universe has to offer. Believe in yourself, and as challenging as it may appear at times, surrender and trust in the process life is presenting to you.

Who you are in this world, and everything you do links to who you believe you are, and subsequently, what you feel you are worthy of having or experiencing.

**"When your self-worth goes up, your net worth goes up with it." ~ Mark Victor Hansen**

The universe does not judge, it simply responds to your beliefs. When you devalue your "self," the universe will give you experiences that match your illusion of unworthiness.

Many of us have doubts that we can be all that we wish to be. We are held prisoner by limiting beliefs that began to form the moment we were born. In truth, with clear intention, focus and persistence, you have the potential to be all that you desire and dare to imagine.

Part of one's quest as a being on earth is to awaken to your authentic self, who you truly are. Acting as a catalyst in this quest, life presents us with challenges, or more accurately, opportunities to connect with your higher self.

When a seed or an acorn is planted, it struggles through the soil to reach the sun. An oak tree grows stronger in the wind. A diamond's sparkle is created under pressure. As humans, we experience undesirable situations, emotional traumas and physical pain, all of which present opportunities to tap into our wisdom, strength and courage so that we may be the light each of us is meant to be.

**Only in darkness**
**can the light of a candle be experienced fully.**

Resisting rather than embracing challenges leads to feelings of heaviness and thoughts of being trapped. Equally true is that one's light is diminished when focused on fears or regrets and in a place of sorrow, anger or non-forgiveness.

When you allow that everything that unfolds in your life is of great magnificence to serve your awakening, you will discover the gem in any circumstance or happening and be stronger for it.

**Be grateful for your precious tears,**
**for they wash the pain away from your soul.**

## Letting Go

**"Letting go may mean coming to the realization that some people are a part of your history, but not a part of your destiny."**

**~ Steve Maraboli**

Many people find it a challenge to let go of what does not serve them. On my journey of awakening, becoming aware of and releasing my illusions and fears about money, lack and self-worth came in a series of life lessons.

Having embraced my spiritual journey, I held a very high standard of perfection as to what a spiritual teacher must represent. I was extremely hard on myself physically, emotionally and spiritually.

As tests of "trust" and "faith" continually presented as challenges in my life, I came to realize that it was impossible to live up to my self-prescribed image. At the darkest of times, I felt forsaken, unheard and alone. I was tired of the struggle, a struggle I came to realize was of my own making.

**Holding a core belief that *spiritual offerings should be free*, I was reluctant to charge for my services.**

Passionate about sharing the inspirational inner knowings that had so touched my heart, I often gifted my classes and workshops to those who seemed unable to afford them. Aware that they desperately needed emotional support, I gifted therapy sessions to those with limited finances.

Putting my need for financial security aside, I adopted a bartering system. My gardening was taken care of, my house was cleaned, and I was the recipient of a great collection of pottery, baked goods and eggs. I began to wonder if live chickens were the next to arrive.

**"If you put a small value upon yourself, rest assured that the world will not raise your price."**

**~ Author Unknown**

As the bartered gifts and services did not pay my bills or mortgage, I kept remortgaging my home until there was not enough equity in my home to secure yet another mortgage. Financially depleted, I feared that I could no longer afford to travel along my spiritual path.

I wondered if it was time to pursue a different career. It saddened me that needing money meant that I might not be able to offer my counseling services and the classes that I'd created and so enjoyed facilitating. With this sadness came a mountain of self-doubt as I asked myself a series of self-diminishing questions.

*Who am I to be teaching?*

*Who am I to offer seminars?*

*Who am I to be a writer?*

*Am I even making a difference in anyone's life?*

*Who am I to think I have gifts to offer the world?*

*What is it that Spirit wants me to realize and accept?*

**"To know your worth**
**is to know the difference between**
**what you're getting and what you deserve."**
**~ Author Unknown**

I had shifted to an unfamiliar paradigm, and I was not happy. There were moments when I felt angry at God and at my guides and angels for abandoning me. Lost and depleted, I felt it was hypocritical to continue my spiritual teachings and questioned my path.

Playing on my mind was the spiritual notion of non-attachment. I wondered whether needing shelter and food was a frowned upon attachment to material goods.

Though I easily accepted that money didn't buy happiness, my state of mind and finances made it abundantly clear that neither did lack of money.

Noticing that, for me, even the word "money" had an emotional charge to it, I questioned, "What is money?" I initially concluded that it is simply a form of exchange, a means for honoring the receipt of goods and services.

**On deeper reflection, I realized that money is *energy* and the highest form of energy is God.**

While in the depth of my fears, I was not able to see clearly. In anguish, I cried out to Spirit, "Please help me figure out what am I meant to do." Instantly, I heard a loud voice inside my head:

**"Let go and value your worth."**

Unable to see the value in my worth, I wondered, "Is Spirit trying to tell me to do something else?"

Collapsing to my knees, through tears, I reached out to Spirit and said, "I surrender it all over to you...my home, my possessions, my life."

As I let go, I felt an incredible weight lift from me.

**By making the choice to surrender, I learned that attachment is what binds one to suffering.**

## STORY: Validation Through a Phone Call

Moments after I surrendered to Spirit, the phone rang. The call was from a woman who had attended one of my talks. Below is what she shared after we exchanged hellos.

"Hannelore, when I was at your seminar a few months ago, you asked, 'If you only had a few months to live, would you feel complete?' I'd never attended this type of seminar before, so I was quite surprised when I heard this very loud resounding voice inside my head scream, 'No!'

You then said, 'If your answer was no, ask yourself what it would take for you to feel complete?' Before I tell you the answer I received, I would like to share something with you.

Twenty-five years ago, I gave birth to a son. Because of my circumstances at that time, I had to give him up for adoption. It tore me apart. I have never spent a day not thinking of him and wondering if he is still okay. I never had any other children, and I was always afraid to look for him in case he didn't want to see me. I was also afraid that he might have died.

When you asked us what it would take to feel complete, I received a very clear message that I was to find him. I am calling to let you know that when I registered to look for him, his name was already on the registry. He was trying to find me!

Since then, we've had many long and wonderful phone conversations, and I'm going to see him next week. I am so excited, and feel a joy I've never felt before.

Hannelore, without you, this would not have happened. I called to thank you and to let you know what a difference you have made in my life."

Tears streamed down my cheeks as my heart burst with joy for her. Feeling a deep sense of gratitude, I immediately gave thanks to Spirit for answering my prayers and for allowing me to be part of the process of this woman connecting with her child. It was the validation I needed. Going forward, if I was to accomplish nothing else, I felt blessed to have helped another being.

In that moment of deep gratitude, I learned to trust that when I ask Spirit for direction with my heart wide open, I will receive the answer.

**I then heard Spirit gently say to me,**
**"Be patient, my child, you will be provided for."**

Hearing those whispers from Spirit, I understood that to surrender is to release any attachment to an outcome. In other words, I realized that to surrender means letting go of the need to control my life circumstances. **It meant letting go of the illusion that I even had control.**

In my surrendering, I finally learned to value my worth. Although I no longer barter services and goods in exchange for attending my classes and workshops, I continue to gift my time to those in need.

I came across this lovely poem "**The Awakening**" by **Sonny Carroll**. It spoke to me and described what I'd just gone through.

**"There comes a time in your life when you finally get it.**

**When in the midst of all your fears and insanity**
**you stop dead in your tracks and somewhere the**
**voice inside your head cries out,**

**'ENOUGH!**
**Enough fighting and crying or struggling to hold on.'**

**And like a child quieting down after a blind tantrum,**
**your sobs begin to subside,**
**you shudder once or twice,**
**you blink back your tears and through a**
**mantle of wet lashes you begin to look at the**
**world from a new perspective.**

**This is your awakening."**

**"Your only obligation in any lifetime**
**is to be true to yourself."**

**~ Richard Bach**

## Do You Feel Complete?

Often times, we walk around as though we have blinders on. One day, something occurs, and you realize you can no longer keep doing what you are doing.

*Do you feel like there is something missing in your life?*

*Do you wonder whether to trust your instincts?*

*Do you have a difficult time making decisions?*

*Do you wonder about how to recognize, begin to follow, or authentically live your intended spiritual path?*

If you answered yes to any of the above questions, trust that **you are awakening to your higher self.**

To continue awakening, make a practice of noticing what resonates with you. It is in your noticing that you will tap into a higher awareness.

Be open to synchronicities, the seemingly coincidental occurrence of related events or happenings. When you trust in the noticing of synchronicities, your higher self will guide you. For when you are open and ready, the universe complies.

**There is something YOU are meant to do. And when you recognize this, the magic of the universe unfolds.**

**"The moment one definitely commits oneself,
then providence moves too.
All sorts of things occur to help one
that would never otherwise have occurred.
Unforeseen incidents, meetings and material
assistance, which no man could have dreamed
would have come his way."
~ Johann Wolfgang von Goethe**

*Do you value your worth?*

*Are you doing what you love to do?*

*Do your close relationships continue to serve you?*

**If your answer to any of the questions above was no, then ask yourself, "Why am I doing this?"**

As I stand before an audience sharing my journey and the simple yet powerful tools that made and continue to make a positive difference in my life...my heart soars, my light shines, and I feel radiant. It does not mean that the "my" truth that I share from my heart is the only way or the absolute right way. I simply know that what I share is right for me and trust that it might help others.

I feel such joy whenever I am witness to another's life transforming in new and wondrous ways. It excites me that a single transformation in one person's life creates a powerful ripple effect, and that every ripple has infinite possibilities as to how many others it touches as an awakening is gifted forward.

**I had to have a car accident and be financially depleted before I understood this.** I now trust my experiences and lessons hold value in that they may shed some light for you so that you may recognize your purpose, your intended path, with ease and grace.

**What you do and who you are in every moment is linked to your *belief*s about your identity.**

There are many wonderful spiritual teachers to help you on your journey of awakening. If you were to ask me about my teachings as they relate to my spiritual path, my response would be, **"I am here to help you remember the authentic essence of who you are."**

For it is within this *consciousness* of your authentic self that you recognize your unique qualities...the gifts inherent in your being that are your innate birthright and have been patiently waiting to be remembered.

**Collectively and globally, as a human race, may we all return to the light and remember our authentic selves.**

**"The impermanent truth of the smaller self can be absurdly unpleasant.**
**Becoming aware of our own misery can be extremely painful, but it is absolutely necessary.**
**We must face the transitory truth of the smaller self as we travel along the path towards the permanent truth of the real self.**
**Often it is necessary to live the joys and sorrows of human love in order to open up space for divine love."**

**~ Sri Prem Baba**

*You deserve all the universe has to offer.*

*Believe in yourself and trust in the process.*

*Know that everything you desire is within you.*

**"You see things as they are, and you say, 'Why?'**
**But I dream things that never were, and I say, 'Why not?'"**

**~ George Bernard Shaw**

## AWAKENING PROCESS

***Do You Feel Complete?***

I invite you to try the following grounding exercise as you connect with your higher self, the eternal spirit essence of who you really are, so that you may hear the whispers of your soul.

Sit in a comfortable chair in a quiet area where you won't be interrupted. Close your eyes and take several long, deep breaths.

To ground, visualize sending imaginary roots from the bottom of your feet into the earth.

Sit quietly and allow your thoughts to just be.

Keep your focus on your breath and relax your body.

After a couple of minutes, ask yourself, **"If I only had a few months to live, would I feel complete?"**

If in your deepest truth, your answer is yes, congratulations! If your answer is no, ask yourself, **"What would it take for me to feel complete?"**

Allow whatever thoughts, feelings and insights you have to come through.

I also invite you to reflect upon your answers and record any whispers from your soul in a journal.

# CH 3: Divine Identity – Your Authentic Self

***Who are you really?***

***What is your divine identity?***

If you believe you are anything less than divine perfection—and this includes the perfection of your perceived imperfections—then you are holding onto a *false* identity.

According to many philosophers, the "self" is pure awareness and pure consciousness. It is not the ego, not just the mind, or just the body, but a oneness with God, Source, the All That Is.

This is your divine self—your authentic self.

According to an article in Wikipedia, "Awareness is the ability to directly know and perceive, to feel, or to be cognizant of events. More broadly, it is the state of being conscious of something."

**Your soul, your inner voice,**
**whispers to you through the voice of your intuition.**

You are far greater than you can imagine. Trusting and believing in your intuition is directly linked to your identity, and to your trust and belief in yourself. Allow your awareness to listen to, recognize and learn to trust and distinguish the voice of your intuition from the many false voices of fear, doubt and indecision.

Most of us hold onto an *illusion of a false identity* of who we really are, which then rules our lives. All of your decisions, relationships, career choices, your neighborhood and home, how much money you have, what and who you attract into your life, are directly impacted by who you perceive yourself to be and what you believe you are worthy of receiving.

**Everything you invite into your life directly correlates with the *vibration* of your beliefs about your perceived identity.**

If your vibration is that you are not worthy, the likelihood of you attaining the experiences you desire will be greatly diminished. Instead, you will attract into your life events and circumstances that reflect your feelings of unworthiness.

When you recognize, define and honor who you truly are, you will realize you are one with the universe and capable of creating whatever you desire in your life. You will know that you are worthy of all the miracles and magic this universe has to offer, and your experiences will be an unfolding of your desires.

**"The first glimpse of truth can be a great darkness. In order to access the truth of who we are, first we must free ourselves from any false identity. It is fundamental on the path of truth that we identify our imperfections or the unpleasant truth about ourselves. So, when we have the humility to recognize and accept our imperfections without wanting to be beyond them, we are ready for the greater truth."**

**~ Sri Prem Baba**

## The Meaning of Self-Actualized

Self-actualized people recognize and maximize their full potential. They have healthy self-esteem, self-respect and honor all of life. They are positive, compassionate, loving, practice gratitude, and express wisdom. They see opportunities rather than problems and find solutions to serve all. They are creative, intuitive, and independent. They are spontaneous and ultimately make positive differences in their own lives, the lives of others, and for the world as a whole.

## Realizing Your Full Potential

**The time of the lone wolf is over.** You have been given the gift of your physical eyes to see outside yourself and to observe what occurs around you. As an observer, you have likely witnessed unfortunate circumstances and happenings that you wish were different. ***But have you acted?***

If you have not acted, perhaps there remains a portion of your soul's intended path that you have yet to recognize.

**Your soul expresses itself through compassion, wisdom and LOVE.**

You hold the unique pieces of a kaleidoscopic journey of awakening that will unlock your mission, your soul's purpose on earth, so that you may realize the self, the oneness with the All That Is.

**When you transcend the illusion of the "one" self, you will discover we are all One.**

I invite you to reach out and connect with others so that we may become one and collectively spread the light on this planet.

**"AND the only miracle that is possible is to enter this Garden of Eden again, to become childlike to allow nature its flow. Don't block it, don't stand in the way, don't push it, just flow with it. You are nature, you are Tao, and you are part of the continuous mystery that is happening."**

**~ Osho**

## Story: She Really Knew!

A number of years ago, I spoke with a young girl in her mid-teens. We were enjoying a deep discussion on spirituality and life in general. She was keenly interested in learning more. Partway through our conversation, I said to her, "You realize you can do anything you want to if you believe you can and know what it is that you want to do."

She replied, "I know!"

Her immediate and confident response surprised me. What so amazed me was her "knowing."

In that powerful moment, I knew she knew! She really got it!

Other times, when I've mentioned the same sentiment to someone, the reply I received was often "I know," but it sounded flat. It was clear to me that they really did not embody or believe that they could do anything they set out to do. Much like when you ask someone how they are, and they robotically reply, "I'm fine, thanks," there was an energy missing in most everyone's response. None was fully connected to the self.

But this girl knew! She fully embodied this truth. I remember thinking, "Wow! She will be successful and accomplish a great deal in her life."

## To Have Self-Realization is to "Realize" the Self by "Realizing" Your Full Potential

Why is it some people are successful and others not?

When you pause and observe someone who is extremely successful, you will notice many qualities, including that she or he has a uniqueness and that uniqueness is obvious. Accomplished people exude confidence and seem powerful. Watching them, one imagines that they have an abundant supply of internal strength, are extremely focused and incredibly determined.

When observing someone who has endured numerous failures, often what is most noticeable is that person's lack of confidence. If you were to chat with that person for a while, you'd likely discover that they have numerous doubts.

### The Falsehood of Doubt

**Doubts about one's ability to succeed and doubts of one's worthiness are directly linked to a doubt of the powerful divine essence inherent in every being. This then creates the illusion of a false identity and results in false blocks that keep you from moving forward on your soul's intended path.**

Take a moment and notice who you hang out with. Are they positive and optimistic, or do they complain and dwell on the negative?

**"If you hang out with chickens, you are going to cluck.**
**If you hang out with eagles, you are going to fly."**
**~ Steve Maraboli**

The universe is infinite in its potential. You have within you the ability to *be*, *do* and *have* anything you desire. Anything! Even that which seems beyond the scope of your wildest imaginings is possible, maybe even walking on water.

## Story: Walking on Water

Life leads one down many paths. Toward the end of my "dark night of the soul" period following my car accident, I spent three years living alone in a remote area of British Columbia.

In addition to the trauma of the head injury I endured in the accident, all four of my beloved family pets passed in less than six months, my romantic relationship ended, and my business faltered to the point where I closed the doors and sold my home. As my grown children had moved on with their lives, I was also experiencing the loss of empty nest syndrome.

During my three-year seclusion, I deepened my spiritual studies. I read voluminous uplifting spiritual books, meditated and reflected on the many words of wisdom from great masters.

With nature at my doorstep, I daily savored the various trails through spectacular and rugged wilderness. Hiking was my favorite form of meditation.

**I feel in the depth of my heart that *nature* is the *divine force* made visible.**

I often hiked many miles up and down valleys. One day as I was completing a familiar circular route, I came upon a stream. I had been there before and often crossed to the other side by hopping on boulders. This day, the stream was more like a river. There was no way to cross without getting my boots wet, and there wasn't enough daylight to return the way I'd come. If I removed my boots, I risked slipping on the many jagged rocks beneath the water.

It was a glorious sunny day, and my heart filled with joy as I drank in many deep breaths of pure sweet mountain air. I welcomed the challenge of crossing the stream as I reflected on the many empowering Bible passages I'd read. Recalling that Christ demonstrated walking on water and said whoever believes in Me can do all that and more, I decided I too could walk on water. Keeping my hiking boots on, I took several long strides into the stream.

**Sploosh, sploosh, sploosh.**

Okay, I came to terms with the fact that I was not fully aligned with that belief just yet!

The actual quote is in John 14:12 and states:
**"Truly, I say to you, whoever believes in me will also do the works that I do; and greater works than these will he do, because I am going to the Father."**

When I first started teaching, the little voice inside my head questioned, "Are you listening to what you are sharing, Hannelore?" It was a gentle nudge and reminder to continue practicing what I was teaching. Even as I write this book, I keep getting a few of these gentle reminders. Whenever I do, I smile as the following thought lovingly and compassionately comes to me: **"Here, take my advice; I am currently not using it."**

It was and remains important for me to be authentic.

**To be authentic is to be**
**genuine, trustworthy, reliable and dependable.**

## Are You Authentic?

To connect to your authenticity, place your compassionate awareness on what you think and do each moment, be it good, bad, downright horrid, or pure brilliance. Do not go into judgement, simply observe. Allow yourself to embrace your authenticity.

**"I yam what I am," said Popeye the sailorman.**

Your consciousness forms while you are in utero. From the moment you are born, you constantly evolve into the person you are today by mimicking the world around you. You first take on the perceptions and beliefs of your parents, and then the rest of your family, friends, and teachers. These influences coupled with your interpretations of your personal experiences create the illusion of your identity. Through this process, you forget who you really are.

In his book *Autobiography of a Yogi*, Paramahansa Yogananda quoted **Shankar—"Knowledge cannot spring up by any other means than the inquiry: Who am I?"**

## AWAKENING PROCESS

***Who Am I?***

I invite you to take a moment and ask yourself the following questions and record your reflections in a journal.

- Who am I?
- Am I this physical body?
- Am I my emotions?
- Am I my thoughts and beliefs?
- Am I my health or dis-ease?
- Am I who I believe myself to be?
- Am I who my family and friends believe me to be?
- Am I my relationships?
- Am I what I do in the world?
- Who was I before I was born?
- Where will I go when I die and who will I be?

There comes a time in everyone's life when we ask ourselves the questions in the previous awakening process. Something deep inside each of us connects with a knowing that there is something greater than ourselves as we strive to understand our purpose.

At the moment you deeply search for the truth and become motivated to maximize your full potential, your journey toward being "self-actualized" begins.

To realize the self is to surrender into silence as you tune into awareness and the awareness of thoughts. As you release these thoughts, you may experience a gentle silence that allows awareness to be just that.

As you place your awareness on your awareness, it is then that you are on your path to self-realization and your relationship with Source. You feel this in the depth of your heart.

**"YOU must be the light you wish to see in the world."**

**~ Buddha**

## Your Physical Body

Einstein, the forerunner of quantum physics, demonstrated to us that our bodies are an illusion. Although we identify and relate to what we can see and touch, we and the world around us are not solid matter. What we view as matter is actually energy.

Although up to 90% of one's body comes from water and an adult body is actually up to 60% water, the body is 99.9999999% empty space. The remainder 0.00000001% that we see or experience as matter is empty space as well. In fact, the entire universe consists of space.

Everything we "see," including ourselves, consists of atoms and the subatomic particles that are the basic units of matter. These atoms and particles are all spinning around in what consists of almost entirely empty space. Yet space is not really empty; it is filled with invisible quantum fields and wave functions.

## Story: Infinitely Small and Infinitely Large

I was raised in a remote and small seaside town on the Pacific Coast of Vancouver Island. As a child, I spent many hours exploring tidal pools and was fascinated at how much life existed there. I often felt like a massive giant peering into another world. As I looked up to the sky, I imagined that our whole planet was like a giant tidal pool with even bigger giants peering at us.

I'd then stare at my hands, arms, legs and feet, and think of the many trillions of cells, molecules and atoms inside my body and imagine how I must be like a giant to them. In my curiosity and wanting to understand what and who God was, I wondered if I and everyone else were cells, atoms and molecules in God's body, the biggest giant of all. Okay, I had a vivid imagination.

## AWAKENING PROCESS

***Unified Water Droplets***

I invite you to consider the ocean as one vast divine being.

Next, imagine that you and I and the billions of other people on the planet are all part of the ocean's unified body of divine water.

Now, imagine each of us being removed one drop at a time and becoming separate droplets that are then birthed into human bodies with individual consciousness.

Further imagine that we coexist in this separated state for a while. But despite that there is a collective link among the droplets to a higher self, the divine self, we feel alone, lost, and as though something is missing.

Now imagine our individuated water droplets are placed back into the ocean. We are no longer separate drops; instead, we have again melded into the one unified body of divine water. **We have all integrated, as have our higher selves, and have become One with the All That Is.**

Following your imaginings, I also invite you to record any thoughts, feelings, insights, questions and/or whispers from your soul in a diary.

**"The man who has no imagination has no wings."**
**~ Muhammad Ali**

The moment we raise our consciousness as a whole, dissolving into Oneness, where no one is greater or less than the other, there is no separation. When judgment and fear are replaced with acceptance, forgiveness and love, and when wars are replaced with peace, then we and this beloved planet, this microcosm, will become one with the macrocosm, the universe.

## AWAKENING PROCESS

***Becoming Aware of Who You Truly Are***

**To evolve, one must pause and turn inward.** I invite you to gently with non-judgment and in your deepest truth**, reflect on who you are, how you perceive your current situation, and your life in general.**

Allow for the presence of the moment. Direct your attention to your "awareness." Whatever thoughts may come and go, simply be aware.

Next, **place your awareness on your "self" as a divine being on this planet.** Then, to really "see" who you are, place your awareness on "who" is aware.

I also invite you to record any thoughts, feelings, insights, questions and/or whispers from your soul in a diary.

## Story: Unexpected Divine-Inspired Guidance

An experience at a workshop I was facilitating left me feeling blessed and in huge gratitude to be of service. The purpose of one of the awakening processes was to allow for the release of blocked emotions while creating a safe space for a connection of pure love.

Sitting in dyads, participants were involved in a powerful breathing technique while gazing into each other's eyes and listening to unrehearsed guidance from me. Below are the divine-inspired words that were unexpectedly whispered through me.

"See the light within your eyes, as you are the light. Look into each other's eyes. Look past the fear, anger and grief, and through the veils of illusion into the light within. Your eyes are the windows to your soul. As you feel this truth in your heart, you will have returned home. As you allow your awareness to acknowledge your breath, you will come to realize that God is breathing with you; and as you tune into the beat of your heart, you will know it to be the heartbeat of God – for you are One.

In the moment that you see the divinity in another, the Oneness, you have both returned home with the complete Oneness of Love for each other and the Oneness with the All That Is. It is then that you have truly embraced the light."

**We are a part everything that is**
**infinitely small and infinitely large;**
**we are One with the Universe—with God.**

**On our shared journey of awakening,**
**to truly "see" One another,**
**we must look past One another's humanness**
**so that we may wholeheartedly embrace**
**One another's divineness.**

Following is a poem that reflects what I feel in my heart. Enjoy.

## The Invitation

**~ Oriah Mountain Dreamer**

"It doesn't interest me what you do for a living.
I want to know what you ache for, and if you
dare to dream of meeting your heart's longing.

It doesn't interest me how old you are.
I want to know if you will risk looking like a fool for love,
for your dreams, for the adventure of being alive.

It doesn't interest me what planets are squaring your moon.
I want to know if you have touched the centre of your own
sorrow, if you have been opened by life's betrayals or have
become shrivelled and closed from fear of further pain.

I want to know if you can sit with pain, mine or your own,
without moving to hide it or fade it or fix it.

I want to know if you can be with joy, mine or your own,
if you can dance with wildness and let ecstasy fill you
to the tips of your fingers and toes without cautioning us to be
careful, to be realistic, or to remember the
limitations of being human.

It doesn't interest me if the story you are telling me is true.
I want to know if you can disappoint another to
be true to yourself;
if you can bear the accusation of betrayal and
not betray your own soul.

I want to know if you can be faithless and therefore trustworthy.
I want to know if you can see beauty even
when it's not pretty every day,
and if you can source your life from God's presence.

I want to know if you can live with failure, yours and mine,
and still stand on the edge of a lake and shout to
the silver of the full moon, "Yes!"

It doesn't interest me to know where you live
or how much money you have.
I want to know if you can get up after the night of grief and
despair, weary and bruised to the bone,
and do what needs to be done for the children.

It doesn't interest me who you are, how you came to be here.

I want to know if you will stand in the centre of the fire with me<br>and not shrink back.<br>It doesn't interest me where or what or<br>with whom you have studied.<br>I want to know what sustains you from the inside<br>when all else falls away.

I want to know if you can be alone with yourself, and if you truly<br>like the company you keep in the empty moments."

# CH 4: Intuition – The Gentle Voice of Your Soul

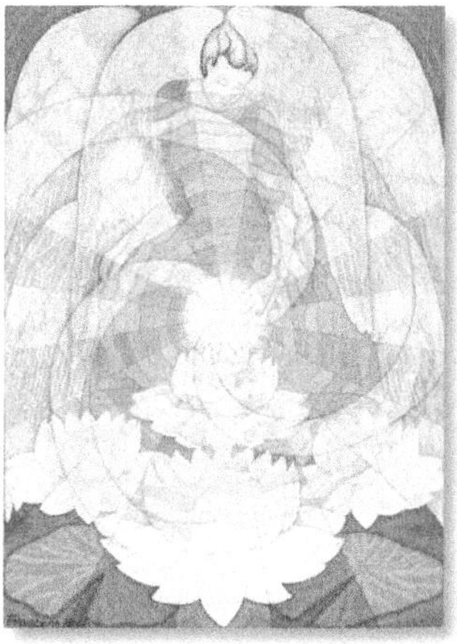

According to the *Webster Dictionary*, "Intuition is a quick and ready insight, an immediate apprehension or cognition, the act or process of coming to direct knowledge without reasoning or inferring."

Intuition, however, is infinitely more than a sudden and certain knowing—it is the gentle voice of your soul. It is a way of knowing and sensing the truth without explanation.

**Intuition is your greatest asset.**
**It's the non-rational, instinctive knowing that provides you with inner guidance,**
**greater intelligence, and wisdom through**
***heart consciousness.***

The word "intuition" is derived from the Latin word, "intueri," which means to "see within."

An intuitive knowing often begins with an initial thought that is followed by the rapid succession of many related thoughts. It is sometimes difficult to distinguish the initial thought from the group of thoughts that may form an intuitive knowing.

Rather than manifest as a thought or groups of thoughts, intuition may instead manifest as sensations in your body. These may be feelings of warmth in the region of your heart or back, tingling sensations in your abdomen, or as goosebumps along your limbs.

**You will recognize the voice of intuition,**
**for it is positive and loving in its subtle urging**
**for you to be all that you can be.**

At times, it may be difficult to fully understand or hear what your intuition is trying to communicate to you. This is because most of us have been conditioned to pay attention to the false voices of fear, doubt and indecision. These false voices create emotional and intellectual barriers that prevent you from trusting your true inner voice, your intuition.

Your intuition provides clarity, strength and purpose as it guides you toward comprehending your inner world. When you learn to silence your mind and *listen to* and *trust* your inner voice, you will be able to look past fear, anger and grief. By doing so, you will see through the veils of illusion into the light within, your inner light.

Your inner light is where you will find the peace, love and answers you seek—they are within you, always were and always will be, moment by moment.

It is when you find this peace within, and only then, that will you realize the peace and love that surrounds you. Once you have experienced this inner light of knowing, even if for a brief moment, you will know your soul's intended path. For it is then that you will completely embrace the brilliance of your being.

Having remembered who you truly are, your gift of intuition will unfold in ways that will continue to amaze you every day.

**"The intuitive mind is a sacred gift and**
**the rational mind is a faithful servant.**
**We have created a society that honors the servant**
**and has forgotten the gift."**
**~ Albert Einstein**

We all have the innate, powerful and creative ability of intuition; yet, we have not been taught how to cultivate it. Our intuition is only as effective as our trust and belief in self.

**Intuition is your higher self**
**speaking from the heart, quietly trying to**
**penetrate the incessant chatter of the mind.**

Your intuition guides you with insights on how to live your life, raise a family, find a career path, and to recognize and cultivate opportunities. It comes in through awareness of synchronicities and inner guidance that help you discern what a truth is and what it is not.

> **"You have to leave the city of your comfort and go into the wilderness of your intuition. What you'll discover will be wonderful. What you'll discover is yourself."**
>
> **~ Alan Alda**

## Story: A Lesson in Trusting My Inner Voice

Have you ever heard and ignored or argued with a whisper, the voice inside your head that tells you to do something? I have, especially when the whisper didn't make sense.

One of the times that I argued with an intuitive whisper happened while I was attending a seminar offered by a colleague who was also a dear friend of mine. We hadn't seen each other for over five years, and I was looking forward to hearing about her life and sharing a few highlights in mine.

Knowing she would be busy with book signings following her presentation, my plan was to go to the front of the queue and quickly hand her my new *Communing with Dolphins* brochure, which included my new phone number and e-mail address.

After my friend's talk, as I attempted to approach the front of the line, a seminar assistant blocked my path and informed me I would have to wait at the end of the line. It was a long queue, so I decided to connect with my friend at another time.

On my way out of the hotel, I stopped at the ladies' room. Once in the cubicle, I placed my brochure on top of the toilet paper holder.

Upon leaving, I was about to pick up the brochure when I heard a clear and loud voice inside my head say, "Leave it there."

What I heard didn't make sense to me, so I continued reaching for the brochure. Once again and more firmly, I heard: "Leave it there!" Using my inner voice, I questioned: "Why would I leave my brochure on a toilet roll holder?" Again, I heard: "Leave it there!" Thinking this was all very weird, I left the brochure where it was as I wondered about who might go into the cubicle next.

The following month, while giving readings at a trade show, a woman sat down in the chair across from mine and excitedly shared that she'd been looking forward to meeting me. She then told me that she was attending a convention in a nearby building and had mentioned to a friend that a lifelong dream of hers was to swim with wild dolphins. Her friend told her that the "Dolphin Lady" was giving readings in the building next door, so she'd come to meet me. Toward the end of her zestful introduction, she said, "I was at a convention in Vancouver last month, and I picked up your brochure. And here you are!"

My curiosity piqued, I said, "I don't remember leaving my brochures at a convention in Vancouver." An instant later, I recalled the whispers of my inner voice urging me to leave my brochure in the ladies' room cubicle. This woman was the one who was meant to find it—we were destined to connect.

**"Intuition is far more powerful than the logical mind."**

**~ Albert Einstein**

Intuition is an "inner knowing" and is a voice of understanding. It does not need to be taught as it is an inherent gift. It may be a "gut feeling" or hunch that something is not quite right. Or you may, seemingly out of nowhere, know how to solve a problem or suddenly "know" what decision to make.

The voice of your intuition may present as a caution, a question or an urging, such as:

> Remember your umbrella.
> Double-check to be sure all the doors are locked.
> Did you turn off the stove?
> You should phone so-and-so.

With practice, one can cultivate and enhance this gift. It is especially powerful when you access your divine wisdom. As you experience and cultivate your intuitive wisdom, you can transcend that which seems impossible.

**Intuition may feel like there is something tugging at your heart, a whisper from your soul that says:**

***"Live your purpose before it's too late. You are here for much grander things than this!"***

## Story: Whispers of Inner Wisdom

My husband, two-year-old son and I moved from the city into an abandoned homestead on a remote 160-acre property in Northern B.C. We had no electricity, phone or indoor plumbing. Until we dug a new well, our water source was a nearby creek. An industrious family of beavers regularly dammed the creek. Almost on a daily basis, we had to dismantle the dam. Although removing the mass of replanted small shrubs and trees, sticks, leaves and mud was a lot of work, I now fully understand the saying "busy as a beaver."

Winter that year was bitterly cold with temperatures averaging minus forty. Thankfully, the oil barrel drum that had been converted into a heater and the woodstove kept our house warm.

Every two weeks, my husband and I travelled forty-five miles to the nearest town for supplies. Half of this distance was gravel logging roads.

In early March, I was six months pregnant and had yet to connect with a local physician. I was experiencing minor abdominal pain and spotting, so we made a trip to town and found a family doctor. Rather than examine me, the doctor suggested I return if the spotting continued. I mentioned that we lived a fair distance away, but he assured me all would be fine.

We were about to head back home, when a voice in my head said, "Drive to the hospital so that you know where it is." Although I immediately felt a sense of urgency, I brushed off what I'd heard. My inner voice continually repeated the instruction and became louder. A few minutes later, I turned to my husband and suggested we check out the hospital before heading home.

As we pulled into the hospital parking lot, I heard the voice again, "Go inside and check out the maternity ward." It was late in the day, so I ignored what I'd heard in favor of going home. But as we started to drive away, the voice persisted, "Go to the maternity ward." Heeding the voice, I told my husband I wanted to go inside and check things out.

Once on the maternity ward, I walked over to the window of the nursery hoping to see the newborns. The only baby in the nursery was in an incubator and had obviously been born prematurely. Thinking of the mother, I thought, "How sad it must be to give birth to a baby that is too tiny and fragile to hold."

Although I had a sense that something was wrong and that I shouldn't leave the hospital, wanting to get home before dark, I ignored my inner wisdom.

During the drive home, I experienced more abdominal pain but assumed it was due to our long and busy day. Shortly after midnight, my contractions were two minutes apart. Despite that I wasn't due for three months, there was no denying that our baby was about to enter the world.

With the narrow roads still partially snow-covered and icy, my husband and I were grateful to know the exact route to the hospital. The universe provided an excellent young doctor whose specialty was dealing with premature births, and our precious baby girl was born healthy and without any major complications.

Over the years, as I learned to cultivate my intuitive skills and to listen to the whispers of my soul, I came to recognize the foreshadowing and guidance I received the day my daughter was born. The urgings from my inner voice kept me safe by insisting that I locate the hospital. Seeing the premature baby was a gentle hint of what was to come. Although I completely ignored my knowing that something was wrong, and that I should stay at the hospital, my inner wisdom had been clear and correct.

The teaching methods of most public schools in North America, and in many countries around the world, are designed so that students use linear and rational thought, which takes place in the left hemisphere of the brain. With the exception of music and art classes, functions that encourage right-brain creative, imaginative and intuitive thinking are not taught. In our innocence as young children, we are steered away from the very essence of who we are, and are often left doubting or ignoring our intuitive gifts.

**"All the works of man have their origin in creative fantasy. What rights have we then to depreciate imagination."**

**~ C.G. Jung**

If you were blessed with supportive and understanding parents, teachers or close friends who encouraged you to be imaginative and creative, you will most likely have learned to trust your intuition and how to use intuitive discernment. Praised for being your authentic self, you most likely have healthy self-esteem and are living your purpose.

## Story: Early Intuitive Training

My German-speaking family immigrated to Canada when I was quite young. While learning the language, Mom often referred to an object that she had yet to learn the English word for as "that thing."

Sometimes she would ask, "Could you get me that thing?" If I didn't immediately know what she wanted, in frustration, she'd say, "You know, that thing! That thing!" As often happens when someone is learning a new language, she would say part of "that thing" in German and part in English and add an "s." So "that thing" became "das dings," with the latter word sounding very much like "dinks."

You can imagine my embarrassment whenever my mother repeatedly said what sounded like "das dinks" in front of my little friends. I soon learned to intuitively discern what it was she wanted so that she didn't have to ask twice.

Many years later, I discovered that the intuitive mind plays a part in helping one to understand what is being said in an unfamiliar language.

> **"Intuition is really a sudden immersion of the soul into the universal current of life, where the histories of all people are connected, and we are able to know everything, because it's all written there."**
>
> **~ Paulo Coelho, *The Alchemist***

## Recognizing Your Intuition

Each of the following questions represent a form of intuitiveness. The more often you answer yes, the more aware you are of your inner wisdom, your intuition.

- When meeting someone for the first time, have you ever had a "gut feeling" that you later learned was accurate?

- Have you ever had an immediate understanding about something for which there was no rational explanation?

- Have you ever had repetitive thoughts, or heard repetitive words in your mind's ear urging you to do something, or cautioning you not do something?

- Have you ever thought of someone you haven't seen for a while, only to bump into or hear from that person within a few days?

- Have you ever felt as though your heart was guiding you?

- Have you ever had an unexplainable feeling or sense that something is about to happen, or that something is amiss with a loved one?

- Have you ever had a premonition or foresight about a coming event or happening that came true?

- Have you ever experienced moments of déjà vu?

- Has your body ever noticeably reacted when you heard a particular sound, smelled something, entered a building or room, or encountered someone? Such reactions might include, but are not limited to, goosebumps, stomach flutters, body rushes, shivers along your spine, stomachache, headache, nausea, dizziness, and sudden feelings of body tenseness, heaviness or lightness.

- Have you ever had an instant knowing about what to do regarding a conundrum, situation or problem?

If you answered yes to most or all of the above questions, congratulations! You are definitely tuned into the voice of your divine wisdom.

**Your true voice of intuition is a higher wisdom and does not come from your rational mind.**

Intuition is a "force," if you will,
that comes through you rather than from you.
As Obi Wan Kenobi, the Jedi warrior in Star Wars
teaches Luke Skywalker—

***"Remember, the force will be with you always."***

## Do You Trust Your Intuition?

Following are a few scenarios to help you understand whether you truly trust your intuition, your inner wisdom.

If there is an occasion when you ignored your first thought or inclination, only to later wish you'd acted or said what was on your mind, you likely missed a cue from your inner wisdom.

Have you ever chosen a checkout queue based on how quickly you think it will clear and found yourself in the slowest line? The next time you go shopping, you might want to think less and instead go with your first inclination.

Take notice of how often you look to others to help you make decisions. The more this happens, the more you doubt your intuition.

Perhaps you realize you have intuitive abilities that are beyond what society considers normal, and fearing others might view you as weird or flaky, you hesitate to share your inner knowings with family and friends. If this sounds like you, remember that intuition emanates from a place of absolute love.

Some religions and cultures view intuitiveness as less than godly. If you were raised to fear or ignore your intuition but no longer wish to do so, you might want to seek out others who share your trust of the loving and divine voice of your inner wisdom.

Some people acknowledge that they are great at following their gut instincts and are excellent decision makers, but view anything to do with the metaphysical realm as nonsense, including intuition. Neither do these people consider themselves as being "spiritual."

I have several friends who fall into this category, and they are some of the most spiritual people I know!

## Story: The Gift of "Seeing" Spirits

We receive our gift of intuitive wisdom in different ways: some *hear*, some *see*, some *sense*, and some have a *knowing*. Some receive intuition in all forms.

Arlene's gift was "seeing" the spirits of people who had passed to the eternal side. But it terrified her.

Arlene and I enjoyed each other's company but rarely had a chance to visit. When we did connect, we often talked about her gift and other matters related to the spiritual realm. Through our conversations, I came to understand that what frightened Arlene the most was not being able to understand why she was able to see spirits.

During one of our visits, Arlene accompanied me to the clinic where I had booked a healing session. She relaxed in the waiting room while I met with my practitioner. Feeling refreshed after my session, I joined Arlene and noticed that she seemed agitated. I asked her if she was okay, and she replied that she was. Although I wasn't convinced, I didn't probe further. Hopefully, she'd share what was on her mind over lunch at a nearby restaurant.

After we ordered our meals, I again asked Arlene if she was okay. She assured me that she was, but when the food arrived, she said that she couldn't eat. Concerned, I had the waitress place our food in takeout containers, and Arlene and I drove to a nearby beach.

After parking the car, I faced Arlene. She looked terrified. Taking her hands and looking into her eyes, I assured her that she was safe. Her eyes filled with tears. I asked her to close her eyes, take several slow deep breaths, ground, and imagine that layers of white and golden light were surrounding her. When she did, I assured her that she was safe within this bubble of divine light. I then asked her, "What happened in the waiting room?"

She stammered, "There was something there. I felt a strong presence."

"Do you know what that presence was?" I asked.

Still frantic, she replied, "No! And it is here with us now!"

I suggested that she take a few more deep breaths. When I could see she was more relaxed, I said, "Know that you are safe in your divine bubble of light and that I am here with you. Now, telepathically ask the presence to identify themselves."

A moment later, Arlene said, "Her name is Jackie and she is about nineteen years old."

"Good," I said. "Let Jackie know we are here to help her if we can. Then listen for a moment while you let her tell you why she is here."

"She's scared and can't understand what is happening to her and why everyone is ignoring her," Arlene said. "She's surprised that I can feel her presence and that I can now also see her. She said that she was in a bad car accident and did not know that she was no longer alive. She feels alone and frightened."

"Arlene, ask Jackie if she can see a light off in the distance."

"She said she can, but it seems far away."

"Tell her that it is safe to go nearer to the light. Then ask her to look into the light and tell you if she can see anyone."

"She is excited because she sees her grandma and her brother. They both passed away some time ago."

"Tell her that it is okay to go to them, that they are waiting for her."

Smiling, Arlene said, "Jackie's gone! She went to her brother and grandma, and they put their arms around her. She looked really happy when she walked into the light with them. She is not here anymore." Opening her eyes, she looked at me and said, "Thanks, Hannelore. That was so beautiful."

If you are one of the many people with the gift of "seeing" or "hearing" or "sensing" spirits and are frightened by it, I suggest that you locate a local spiritual church or group, and connect with others who are similarly gifted. Know that once you transcend your fear, you will be able to help heal those grieving the loss of a loved one.

## Story: Remember the Bird

Another dear friend has the remarkable gift of receiving messages from the spirit world. Having experienced others' skepticism, whenever she dares to share a message from spirit with an intended recipient, she prefaces it with something such as "This may sound strange, and you can do whatever you want with what I'm about to share, but I had a vision of your departed loved one and he/she asked me to tell you...."

One day while my sister and I were enjoying a long and relaxing visit with this dear friend, I mentioned that my mother was not coping well with our father's passing. I also explained that our parents had spent sixty years together, so losing Dad was extremely difficult for Mom. I then asked my friend if she was open to receiving a message from him, and if she was, could she let us know something we could share with Mom that would be proof that Dad was okay.

My dear friend closed her eyes and took a deep breath. "Your Dad just came in and said, "Tell her to remember the bird.'"

I looked at her questioningly and asked, "The bird?"

She replied, "He is really excited and keeps repeating, 'Tell her to remember the bird, tell her to remember the bird.'" After a short pause, she asked us, "Does what your dad is saying mean anything to either of you?"

Neither my sister nor I could think of anything related to a bird and our parents, and were perplexed that that was the entire message from Dad. Nothing else came through.

The next day, my sister and I met at Mom's place for lunch. She was experiencing a difficult day of grief. Hoping it might help, we told her about our friend's message from Dad.

We were both disappointed when Mom's response was a quizzical, "The bird?" She had no idea what it meant, and left us alone while she went to get something from the kitchen. A moment later, we heard her shout, "I know what it is! Come here!"

When we went into the kitchen, Mom was standing in front of the fridge. Looking much happier, she said, "A number of years ago, your father and I stood right here and discussed the passing of several of our friends. We questioned whether there really was life after death. After all, no one ever appeared and said, 'Hi there, I'm okay.' So, I said to your father, 'If I go before you, I will move this bluebird magnet that is on the freezer door of the fridge.' Your father replied, 'And if I go before you, I will move the bluebird magnet.'"

My sister and I both smiled as Mom exclaimed, "Do you know how many times I came into the kitchen and the bluebird magnet had moved to the other side of the freezer door. I assumed it shifted when I shut the door."

As a test, I opened and closed the freezer door several times. The bluebird magnet did not budge.

Mom asked, "How would he remember that?"

"How did you just remember that?" I asked.

Smiling wide, she said, "As I walked up to the fridge, I spotted the bluebird magnet and suddenly remembered our conversation in the kitchen as though it happened yesterday."

My dear friend had no way of knowing that my parents had made a pact that whoever parted first would reach out to other via the moving of the bluebird magnet. It would be a stretch for even the most skeptical person to attribute her message from my father as being mere coincidence or hogwash.

My dearly beloved mother has since passed. I now have the bluebird magnet on my fridge door. Each time I look at it, I'm grateful that my mother and father are watching out for me and the rest of our family from the other side.

## The Heart's Emotional Intelligence

Commonly called *emotional intelligence* and sometimes referred to as *heart math*, the human heart has its own profoundly intelligent brain, which works together with the cranial brain. This heart intelligence is a rapid conduit to accessing one's subconscious and intuition. This allows for precognitive knowings when a future event is emotionally relevant.

The HeartMath Institute describes the heart as: "Personal coherence, also known as psychophysiological coherence, refers to the synchronization of our physical, mental and emotional systems. It can be measured by our heart-rhythm patterns: The more balanced and smoother they are, the more in sync, or coherent we are."

Gratefully, unlike a few decades ago, we live during a time when it is acceptable to acknowledge, utilize and share insights that emanate from one's intuitive gifts. From personal experience and accounts from others, I know that becoming aware of, cultivating and celebrating one's divine gifts illuminates the soul's intended path. With this mind, I invite you to tune into your heart and ask the universe for your teacher(s) to arrive.

Within a very short while, you'll recognize the help you receive. Your teacher(s) may come in the form of a person, a group of spiritually minded people, a book, or a happening that opens the window to your soul.

**"The more and more each is impelled by that which is intuitive, or the relying upon the soul force within, the greater, the farther, the deeper, the broader, the more constructive may be the result."**

**~ Edgar Cayce Reading 792-2**

## Story: The Art of Intuitive Action

The following is a recap of an inspiring and remarkable story that happened to **Phil Evans**, a motivator and life coach. It is a great example of the art of intuitive action.

One day, Phil's daughter telephoned him. At the time, she was twenty years old and visiting Airlie Beach in Northern Queensland, which was about 2500 kilometers away from where he lived in Newcastle. Through sobs, she told him that she was facing an emotional trauma and feeling isolated and alone. After listening to her for a while, Phil asked her what it was that she needed most. She replied that what she most needed was support and a hug from him.

For some reason he didn't understand, Phil asked his daughter to describe her surroundings. She said she was in public phone booth (one of three) in a small park on the main street of Airlie Beach, and that there were small shops around the park. With a clear picture of where she was in his mind, he then told her that if she didn't hear from him within thirty minutes, she should call him back.

After hanging up, Phil sat for a few minutes as he pondered what to do. A phone number popped into his head that he recognized but couldn't recall whose number it was. When he called the number, a woman who'd bought a house from him eighteen months earlier answered the phone.

According to Phil, his exact words to this woman were, "Oh, it's you, Liz. I have no idea why I'm calling you in particular, but my daughter is stranded in Airlie Beach, and I just got the thought to ring you and tell you that. Have you any idea why?"

Liz responded, "It could be because my son lives there."

After Phil shared what had transpired during his call with his daughter, he asked for Liz's son's cell phone number, and she happily gave it to him. About five minutes had passed since he'd spoken with his daughter.

Phil immediately called Liz's son, and he answered. After explaining who he was, he gave the young man a description of his daughter, told him where she was standing, and shared that she needed emotional support. He then asked Liz's son if he could find it in his heart to help out.

To Phil's surprise, Liz's son said, "I can see her! She is right across the street from where I am standing." He walked up to her and said, "Your dad sent me," and then introduced himself. As the story goes, she responded with something like "Wow! Dad's getting pretty good at this stuff."

Liz's son helped Phil's daughter locate a safehouse where she received the support she needed. She was also given food, a bed for a couple of nights, and enough money to get herself to where she needed to be.

Phil's trust of his intuition may well have saved his daughter's life. At the very least, it allowed him to provide her with the emotional support she needed. *That's intuition at its best!*

**You can learn to easily and confidently make empowering decisions in your personal and business life.**

Intuition is your birthright and a skill that you can develop and enhance. It can help you transcend fears, doubts of self-worth, and abandonment issues that stifle your ability to trust. Intuition can also help to quiet the negative voices of past conditioning.

**"Your time is limited,**
**so don't waste it living someone else's life.**
**Don't be trapped by dogma – which is living with**
**the results of other people's thinking.**
**Don't let the noise of other's opinions drown out**
**your own inner voice.**
**Most important, have the courage to**
**follow your heart and intuition.**
**They somehow already know**
**what you truly want to become.**
**Everything else is secondary."**

**~ Steve Jobs**

***Are you ready to unleash and remember the natural gifts you were born with?***

**The following awakening process will help you do just that!**

## AWAKENING PROCESS

### *12 Ways to Cultivate Your Intuitive Skills*

Following are twelve processes for cultivating your intuitive skills. I invite you to reflect on each one, and where it is suggested, I also invite you to record your reflections in a diary.

1. Practice mindfulness by pausing and being aware of all that is happening around and within you. Using your five physical senses, notice what you hear, see, touch, taste and smell. While letting go of the past and future, and without judgment, notice your thoughts, feelings and body sensations in that very moment. Breathe slowly and deeply as you simply be.

2. If being aware of and trusting your intuition is unfamiliar to you, allow for the possibility that intuition is real and that you can learn to connect with and cultivate it. Imagine ways that your intuition might help you discover your purpose and to live the life you are meant to live.

3. Start an *intuition journal* to record and track intuitive nudges, and make a note as to whether you listened to or ignored them. Notice and record any feelings and body sensations you may have just prior to or immediately after heeding or ignoring your intuition.

4. Connecting with nature will deepen your connection to your divine inner wisdom. Spend time in an outdoor setting. While quietly sitting or standing, feel the earth beneath you, notice the elements in the sky above you, and the sensations of the movement and temperature of the air on your skin.

Close your eyes and listen to nature's varied sounds. Notice the buzz of an insect, a trickle or lapping of water, the song of a bird, the sound of the wind or a nearby animal or rodent.

Spend a few moments communing with a single blade of grass, a flower or plant. Note any sensations in your body as you notice its color, shape, scent and texture.

Place your palms on the bark of a tree. For me, trees resemble "standing people" as they have much to convey through subtle vibrations and whispers.

There is abundant activity and infinite wisdom in nature. Let your intuition guide you to the best place to focus, then allow for an intuitive message to come through.

Be it while in nature, at home, or over your favorite beverage at a nearby café, write your inspirations and intuitions in your journal.

5. Notice when you have a sudden dislike or instant like for someone you meet. Record what you sense or feel in your journal, so that over time, you can notice how your intuition plays out.

6. Make a note of the times when you have a gut feeling about a current situation or upcoming event. It could be an intense feeling, an inner call to pay attention, a premonition, or a knowing about how you respond, act or react.

7. Notice when you receive an intuitive message from the quiet *voice within*. It might come in the form of whispers, thoughts or words.

Listen for the crux and nuances in the message as you determine if you're being *nudged* or *urged* to do or not do something. Sometimes, a sudden knowing is meant to be shared as a nudge with a recipient other than yourself. Other times, it might be an urging to avoid a potentially hazardous circumstance or event.

8. Reflect on the times you ignored your first thought and did *not* act on something.

9. Jot down in your journal what the situation was at times when you acknowledged and trusted your intuitive voice. Ask yourself why the message you heard, thought or felt resonated as being a truth you should acknowledge.

10. Invite a friend to join you to practice cultivating your inner voice. For instance, you might take turns with one person thinking about or drawing an image or number, while the other sees if he/she can determine what it is.

Make an agreement with your friend that when the other comes into your thoughts, you will imagine where that person is at that moment, and jot the time and details in your journal. You might include a description of what your friend is wearing, where they are, and what they are feeling or experiencing.

11. Incorporate cultivating your intuitiveness into your daily routine. For instance, while shopping, intuitively discern which checkout queue will move the quickest. When the phone rings, do your best to discern who it is before you answer or peek at your cell phone screen.

When devising ways to cultivate your intuitiveness, use your imagination and have fun! The possibilities are infinite.

12. By far, the most effective way to cultivate your intuitiveness is by participating in an Intuition Awareness Program. Doing so will accelerate your skills beyond measure as you practice with and learn from like-minded individuals.

**Professional Teachers:** To locate a local group or learn about the offerings of a professional teacher, type "intuitive practice group" into the search bar of your computer. A professional program will help you cultivate and enhance your intuitive skills for you to use in your personal and professional life. Spiritual churches and *Meetup* groups are also excellent for connecting with people interested in developing their intuition.

**Intuition is a *Knowing* Without Knowing Why You Know**

Intuition does not come from reasoning, logic or common sense. Rather, it is the accessing of what might be called *collective subconscious* that exists and emanates from the divine realm.

# CH 5: Intuition in Business

All too often we dismiss our intuition because we have been culturally conditioned to think logically and ignore anything that can be considered as being "woo-woo."

The truth is that intuition is an invaluable innate ability that can help you make wise decisions and choices, personally and professionally.

**"It is through science that we prove,**
**but through intuition that we discover."**
**~ Henri Poincaré**

## Intuition in Business is to Think Outside of the Box

Heeding your intuitive knowings will give your business an "edge" not enjoyed by entrepreneurs who ignore theirs. Originating in the brain's right hemisphere, intuition encourages out-of-the-box thinking and creativity. Businesspeople who rely solely on the logic of left-brain rationale, often miss the emotional cues that lead clients to purchase or not purchase a product or service.

When you are open to intuitively discerned ideas and solutions, problems are more easily solved, clients' needs are more readily identified, and hidden agendas are quickly exposed. Listening to your intuition enriches your communication skills, and helps you identify ideas that will prove lucrative from ones that will fail. Your intuitive intelligence allows you to "sense" pricing strategies and what your customer ultimately needs.

**"My business skills have come from being guided by my inner self - my intuition."**

**~ Oprah Winfrey**

The book *Emotional Intelligence* by Daniel Goleman offers amazing insights about how what we typically view as "intelligence" does not determine our level of success or career fulfilment. One's emotional intelligence plays a far more significant role.

Emotional Intelligence (EI) allows us to identify, manage and clearly express our emotions. It also helps us determine how to handle other people's emotions. Being able to manage our own and others' emotions is a crucial skill for decision makers.

Those with highly developed emotional intelligence have more self-confidence, are more creative, and tend to trust their intuition.

**"Leaders must exemplify integrity and earn the trust of their teams through their everyday actions. When you do this, you set high standards for everyone at your company. And when you do so with positive energy and enthusiasm for shared goals and purpose, you can deeply connect with your team and customers."**

**~ Marillyn Hewson**

In his book *Working with Emotional Intelligence*, when it comes to who's most likely to succeed professionally, Goleman cites Harvard Business School research that shows EI is twice as important as intelligence and technical skills combined. Other studies attribute emotional intelligence as being eighty percent of what it takes to be successful.

Some of the greatest business minds, creators, inventors, and scientists attribute their success to using their intuition, their "inner knower."

**"Intuition is a very powerful thing,**
**more powerful than intellect, in my opinion."**
**~ Steve Jobs**

Whether you refer to this inner wisdom as a "gut feeling," a "hunch" or an "instinct," to ignore one's intuitive awareness is akin to viewing the world with one eye closed.

**Carl Jung noted:**
**"Intuition does not denote something contrary to reason,**
**but something outside the province of reason."**

**Andrew Lo said:**
**"Great investors need to have the right combination of**
**intuition, business sense and investment talent."**

## My Business Background

If you have yet to read the prologue at the beginning of this book, I invite you to do so now.

**I am so very grateful for my intuitive internal antenna.**

Although I wasn't yet fully aware of what I was doing, listening to and trusting my inner voice played a significant role in my success as a model and actress. When I later opened my film industry marketing business, paying attention to my intuition enabled me to easily develop strategies. This led to my exclusive representation of several large production companies and over fifty high-profile directors of commercials.

**And yet, there came a time when I felt something was missing!**

The prologue also chronicles the events that unfolded to catapult me onto my spiritual path, happenings that turned out to be hidden blessings for which I am eternally grateful.

**"We all have possibilities we don't know about.**
**We can do things we don't even dream we can do."**
**~ Dale Carnegie**

Following are a few quotes from accomplished individuals whose words continue to inspire me to trust my intuition, and to know that:

**When you listen to the divine inspired whispers of your soul, the doorway to greatness opens wide.**

Legendary hedge fund tycoon **George Soros**, who regularly invests billions of dollars of his clients' money, candidly shared that "animal instinct" (intuition) is part of his investment strategy. When asked how he knew when the fund's portfolio needed tweaking, he responded:

> **"I feel pain. I rely a great deal on animal instincts. When I was actively running the fund, I suffered from backache. I used the onset of acute pain as a signal that there was something wrong in my portfolio."**

Renowned English poet, novelist, critic and classicist, **Robert Graves** said:

> **"Intuition is the supra-logic that cuts out all the routine process of thought and leaps straight from the problem to the answer."**

**Masaru Ibuka, a cofounder of Japan's Sony Corporation,** was asked if he would share the secret to his success. Ibuka explained that before moving ahead with a business proposition, he would make herbal tea and before drinking it, ask:

> **"Should I make this deal or not?" If the tea gave him indigestion, he wouldn't make the deal. "I trust my gut, and I know how it works. My mind is not that smart, but my body is."**

**Michael Munn, Ph.D.,** an award-winning engineer and former aerospace chief scientist for Lockheed, worked on a program aimed at stopping Russian nuclear bombs in space. He accredited his success to brief daily meditations, which allowed taking the time to listen to his inner knowing and the resulting ignitions. Munn said:

> **"How do I know the answers are there? I see pictures or movies or dreamlike sequences. I have an immediate inner knowing that this is the answer for which I was waiting. My intuition lets me know, 'This is it!'"**

## AWAKENING PROCESS

***Developing Your Intuitive Business Skills***

Following are a number of processes for cultivating your intuitive business skills. I invite you to reflect on each one. I also invite you to record your reflections in a diary.

- Notice when you have a gut feeling, hunch or sudden insight about an employee, client, project, situation or problem.

- Be mindful and fully aware in each moment. Trust that it is your intuition coming through when something feels "right" or feels "wrong."

- Keep track of the various ways your intuition speaks to you by daily recording your observations and knowings in a journal.

- Notice your physical sensations and tune into what a particular feeling is meant to relay. An intuitive nudge to move ahead with an idea may be accompanied by a gut feeling, tingling in your limbs, or a warm rush along your spine. Feeling constricted, shortness of breath or nausea may signal that something is amiss, and you need to take a closer look at a potential hire, a project or client contract.

- Keep track and write down any synchronicities that could possibly relate to your business. (The next chapter in this book examines the differences between a coincidence and a synchronicity.)

- Set an intention to remember your dreams, record them in your diary, and reflect on what your subconscious is communicating. This is particularly important when your waking hours are consumed with tasks that move you away from being mindful and aware of your inner wisdom.

- Fear of failing, self-doubt and indecision are part of the false voice of conditioning. Trust your intuition, surrender your fears and doubts to your higher self, and spend time in nature so that you can fully reconnect with your authentic Self.

- It is possible to take on another's negative energy. If being in someone's company brings you down, where possible, avoid them as they will drain your positive energy and move you away from your inner wisdom. If you're not already aware, you might want to learn about these "energy vampires" and ways to ensure they don't derail you from your intended path.

- Listen to your inner voice and be sure to keep a record of what comes up.

**Meditate, as it is always important to be in the present moment and tune into your inner wisdom. It is when you are in the moment that an *aha* may occur.**

**"Cease trying to work everything out with your minds.**
**It will get you nowhere.**
**Live by intuition and inspiration and**
**let your whole life be Revelation."**

**~ Eileen Caddy**

**"Intuition is the key to everything...in painting, filmmaking, business – everything. I think you could have an intellectual ability, but if you can sharpen your intuition, which they say is emotion and intellect joining together, then a knowingness occurs."**

**~David Lynch**

# CH 6: Synchronicities

***Intuition* is the inner voice of divine wisdom.**

***Synchronicities* are the outer manifestations of the inner voice, the observable events.**

Throughout the many years I've studied and embraced my spiritual journey, much of what I believe is based on *trust*.

I trust there is a God. I trust there are angels and guides supporting us. I trust there is meaningful reason for life on earth, and trust there is an existence beyond death. I trust that we are all One.

**It is the occurrence of multiple extraordinary synchronicities—in my life and others' lives—that cements my absolute faith in the *All That Is* by providing me with tangible proof that my trust is well-placed.**

There is a magnificent divine force beyond the physical realm that is far greater than the rationale mind easily comprehends. But when you listen to the intuitive whispers of your soul, and *allow for*, *observe* and *honor* the unfolding of synchronous occurrences, you witness the earthly manifestation of the All That Is. You will know that not one of us is alone, and that your life on earth has purpose as part of the grander scheme of the universe.

The term "synchronicities" was coined by Carl Jung to denote "meaningful coincidences."

**"Events bound by synchronicity are connected by similarity, by meaning, by resonance, rather than by causality. Synchronicity is an acausal connecting principle. Since it goes beyond causation, it goes beyond time and space, and is not limited by such relations."**

**~ Carl Jung**

According to the *World Book Dictionary*, intuition "is the immediate perception of understanding of true facts or events without reasoning. In other words, it is a 'knowing.'"

**The clear voice of intuition does not come from fear. When one learns to distinguish their voice of intuition from the false voices of fear, doubt and indecision, they are then guided to recognize the outer manifestations of synchronicities.**

A *synchronicity*, sometimes referred to as *serendipity*, often provides validation of an earlier intuitive knowing. In turn, one's intuition often interprets the meaning of a synchronicity. In other words, a synchronicity acts like a guide, a "way show-er," that our intuition deciphers.

As synchronicities sometimes metaphorically present through clues, riddles and symbols, one can't help but know that the soul encourages mindfulness and honors the use of one's imagination.

More than an unexplainable coincidence or a series of coincidences, synchronous happenings are one of many means by which the universe guides and communicates with you. When you intentionally open yourself to *noticing* the synchronicities in your life, you *enhance* your intuition.

> **"There is always a message for you behind any mysterious 'coincidence.' Synchronicity is the language the universe uses to show you the next steps of your journey."**
>
> **~ Sri Prem Baba**

## Story: Book Fell Off the Shelf

I met my very dear friend Jane when I was twenty years old. I watched her precious daughter Susan grow into a lovely young and powerful woman. Unfortunately, their relationship did not fare well. They didn't speak to each other for many years. On one of my visits with Susan, she expressed her difficulty communicating with her mother, then after a deep sigh, she said, "It's impossible."

Later that afternoon, we visited a bookstore to pick up a few items I wanted. As Susan slowly meandered down the aisle, a book fell off a high shelf and she caught it. Although I cannot recall the exact title of the book, I do remember the subtitle was about resolving issues with one's mother.

Albeit a bit shaken by the "weirdness" of the incident, Susan bought the book. I am happy to report that their relationship is now amazing!

## Intuition Plays a Vital Role in the Interpretation of a Synchronicity

As seers and healers, Shamans are trained to recognize and interpret messages from the "Cosmic Intelligence." To do this, they rely on their sixth sense, their intuition, to decipher the metaphoric synchronicities that are being presented.

With practice, conscious awareness, and by tuning into your inner voice of wisdom, you will be guided to recognize the outer manifestations of synchronous events. Within a short while, you'll likely be amazed by the number of synchronicities that occur in your life.

**As synchronicity and intuition enjoy a reciprocal or symbiotic relationship, the more often you recognize synchronicities, the more heightened your intuition.**

There is often a tendency for one's left-brain reasoning to override or doubt the significance of a synchronous event. Once you begin to recognize the numerous synchronicities in your life, your right-brain intuition will easily discern what are truly divine happenings.

Synchronicities can present in infinite ways. For instance, you could be wondering whether to take a course, and within a day or two, a check arrives in the mail for roughly the amount of the course fee. The abandoned search for an item could result in the item suddenly materializing, seemingly out of nowhere.

## Story: The Afterlife of Billy Fingers

During a lovely visit with a friend of mine, I shared several true stories from my forthcoming book, *The Other Side of the Window ~ Communing's from Beyond the Veil.* She excitedly pulled out a book she was reading with similar stories to mine and gifted it to me.

It was titled ***The Afterlife of Billy Fingers*** and was written by Annie Kagan. I brought it with me the following week on my flight to Hawaii, and thoroughly enjoyed reading it. Unfortunately, when I finished unpacking my suitcase in my hotel room, I realized that I'd left the book on the plane.

Once back home, I looked for the book on Amazon. At the time, I couldn't remember the exact title, but knew I would recognize it as soon as I saw it. I was reluctant to phone my friend and ask for the title because I was embarrassed that I'd lost her wonderful gift.

While on Amazon, I spent a very long time looking through many books to do with life after death. When I couldn't find the title I was looking for, I eventually gave up and instead ordered two books for my grandchildren. When I clicked on the checkout icon, there were three items in my cart. Thinking that it was possible that I had mistakenly clicked on one of children's books twice, I proceeded to check out.

To my utter surprise, when I previewed the items in my order, there it was—*The Afterlife of Billy Fingers.* This time, it was a very precious gift from the universe!

> **"The intellect has little to do on the road to discovery. There comes a leap in consciousness, call it Intuition or what you will, the solution comes to you and you don't know how or why."**
>
> **~ Albert Einstein**

Albert Einstein readily acknowledged the significance of his intuition when pondering a scientific quandary. When pondering situations in your life, it is wise to set an intention much like a scientist would identify a query and then set about discerning the answers.

An intention could be a statement about a desired outcome or the attainment of a goal. An intention can also be formulated as a question you ask your guides or higher self as you release all attachment to an outcome.

Once an intention has been set and your attachment to the outcome released, the "how" and/or "why" of a conundrum or goal will present through synchronous happenings and intuitive knowings. The more you are in tune with your intuition, the more you will recognize the blessings of daily synchronicities in your life, gently showing you the way.

Aware of the wisdom in setting intentions, following is a story as told to me by one of my students. It's an excellent example of a synchronicity.

## Story: Student's Quandary

"Before you and I met, Hannelore, I came across your brochure and was considering whether to register for your intuition program. I was having difficulty making the decision and had to make up my mind as the program was to begin in another week. I asked my guides for help and that they give me some kind of sign.

A few days later, I attended an event with hundreds of attendees. During an intermission, I was in a long lineup, and directly in front of me was a group of women who kept mentioning your name as they discussed how your intuition training had changed their lives. Needless to say, it was a very clear sign for me to make the decision to register."

> People regularly misinterpret synchronicities as being mere coincidences when a more logical explanation would indicate that something other than random happenings has occurred.

**Phone Synchronicity:** Think back to the number of times you've thought about someone and that person then called you within a few minutes, hours or days. Have you ever picked up the phone to dial someone only to discover he or she is already on the other end and neither of your phones have rung?

**Traffic Synchronicity:** Have you ever thanked your lucky stars after hitting what seems like every red traffic light on your way to an appointment, only to pass a serious car accident that happened minutes earlier?

**Paths Crossing Synchronicity:** When miles away from home, have you ever been drawn to visit a place or walk down a street and unexpectedly run into an old friend or acquaintance?

**Synchronous Higher Selves Crossing:** Have there been times when you repeatedly meet up with the same person, perhaps at a store, then at the bank and then again while you're both stopped at a traffic light? When this happens, it's quite possible that your higher selves are crossing, and you are meant to connect for an important reason.

The reason may not present itself right away, and instead unfold as one or both of you are ready to know it. If you are not sure of the why behind a synchronous crossing with another, you might ask your higher self for clarification. For example, you could ask, "Why is this person showing up in my life?" Or, "Why am I feeling what I am feeling when I see this person?"

## Story: Wrong Number?

As an ordained minister of the Interfaith Church, I am registered with the city of New York and can legally perform marriage ceremonies throughout the United States. However, as there isn't an established Interfaith Church in Canada where I live, I must have a marriage commissioner witness the ceremony and sign the marriage license. For years, I worked with Pamela, a marriage commissioner and a dear friend.

Unfortunately, Pamela developed breast cancer, had surgery, and then moved to a different area. We lost touch with each other. Over the years that followed, I often tried to connect with her again, but wasn't successful.

My life was also filled with changes, including several moves, a world tour, and relocating to Vancouver. It was early December, and I had just settled into a new home when I was asked to perform a wedding ceremony.

On my Christmas shopping list was the purchase of a one-year membership at a nearby seniors' center for my mother. My son's wife worked at the fitness center located in the same building as the seniors' activity center. With the intention of asking my daughter-in-law to pick up the membership pass, I called my son and asked him for her number at work. He gave me a number, and then said, "I think this is the number, but if it's not, call me back."

I phoned the number and a woman answered. It didn't sound like my daughter-in-law, so I asked if she was there. The woman on other end of the phone said, "No, I think you have the wrong number, but is this Hannelore?" Surprised, I replied, "Yes." To which she said, "This is Pamela."

Now this would be amazing in itself, but there's more.

I said, "Oh my God, Pamela! Are you working at the fitness center?" She explained, "No, this is my new home number. I've been out of the country and just returned late yesterday afternoon. While shopping for a few groceries, I came across a magazine article with your contact information. I was going to give you a call this morning."

**The universe will present you with synchronicity after synchronicity when you get yourself out of the way and allow the divine to shower you with goodness—when you live in the realm of the sacred.**

Many events occur that create threads in the tapestry of our lives. How we weave these threads into the fabric of our existence determines our strength and our *synchro destiny*.

We often don't understand why certain things happen in our lives. For instance, we may not know why we are guided to certain places or to meet certain individuals. But the more you allow for these possibilities, and take that extra moment to tune into your inner voice and ask why, the more you will be surprised at the answers that come forth.

The powers that be will continually guide you to connect with individuals who could potentially have an impact on your life. Although you may not recognize the opportunity in the moment, when looking back at the synchronicity of a connection, it is easy to recognize the impact someone has had on your destiny. Every person you meet could potentially be leading you toward your **divine purpose—to your "synchro destiny."**

**Deepak Chopra defined *synchro destiny* as: "Coincidence containing purpose that has direction and intention."**

Through the intervening of synchronicities, one may be called to expand upon a chosen path or to venture onto an entirely different path. For example, a musician or actor who has successfully followed a path toward stardom might be asked to use her/his celebrity status to help raise funds for underprivileged children in a foreign country. Should this happen, that person's career would take on new meaning. The joining of that person's talent with purpose and intention might seem like a coincidence; however, when you understand the infinite wisdom of the universe, you can't help but wonder if it were destined to be—to know in your heart that such a union is synchro destiny at its finest.

You may think you must head in a particular direction when the universe wants to direct you elsewhere. Perhaps, you'll be guided to an entirely new direction that offers the opportunity for you to meet individuals who could potentially be the catalyst for you to step into your divine essence and purpose.

**Within each and every one of us, there dwells all the wisdom of the universe. Know that this divine guidance is patiently waiting for you to transcend your fear so that it can be revealed in all its glory.**

Even when we are acutely aware that divine guidance presents through intuition and synchronicities, we sometimes miss when the universe has intervened on our behalf. It wasn't until I was writing this chapter that I became aware that destiny-altering experiences in my life were in fact a sequence of synchronicities.

I was stunned by the revelation. These synchronicities stretched over five years, and ultimately led to the fruition of my synchro destiny. I've shared this experience in the following story.

## Story: Dolphin Connection

For several years, I annually attended the Wesak Festival celebrating Buddha's birthday in Mount Shasta, California. After attending one in 1997, I decided it would be my last. But I kept receiving strong intuitive nudges (inner whispers) that it was important to attend one last time.

At the festival the following year, I met Phil who was promoting his home in Maui as a bed-and-breakfast. While looking through his photo album (and as an avid organic gardener) I fell in love with his vegetable garden. I thought that if I was ever to visit Maui, I would rather stay in a place like his than a hotel. We exchanged business cards.

A year and a half later, I registered for a one-week retreat in Maui. As I was making plans for my stay before and after the retreat, I had a strong intuitive nudge to find Phil's card. The memory of our meeting, the photo album, the garden, the B-and-B, and our exchange of cards flashed before my eyes. I searched many hours for his card. Unable to find it, I surrendered and trusted the perfect place would show up. Two days before my flight to Maui, I received a phone call from Phil. He just happened to come across my card and felt the impulse to call.

Phil's telephoning me shortly after I gave up on finding his business card was a profound synchronicity. But what I find even more fascinating was the interweaving of the many subsequent synchronicities that soon unfolded.

Following the Maui retreat, while still on the island, I went swimming at a remote beach. It was then that I first enjoyed a heart opening and deeply moving eye-to-eye communication with a solitary non-captive dolphin. I was delighted by how effortless it was to be in complete harmony with this wonderous creature.

Having just completed a retreat, I knew in that moment that I wanted to share this incredible joy with others and was inspired to create the *Communing with Dolphins* retreat.

My imagination soared as I visualized offering an all-inclusive retreat for small groups where we could live communally in a beautiful house at the ocean's edge. It needed to be a place where I could safely guide participants in and out of the water. Ideally, it would be located on a bay that dolphins frequented.

I asked a number of people if they knew of such a place, but all responded that they didn't. It was suggested that I have groups stay at a hotel and charter a boat or two with the hope that we might encounter non-captive dolphins. This idea didn't resonate with me.

When I later shared my dream with Phil, he told me that his ex-partner catered events at a house on another island that was located right at the edge of a bay that the dolphins often frequented. The warmth radiating in my heart told me what I needed to know—I'd found the perfect spot to make my vision a reality.

I spent the next few years researching dolphin behavior and experiencing many more exciting encounters. The first *Communing with Dolphins* retreat happened in 2003, and I've had the ultimate pleasure of facilitating these magical gatherings every year since.

*Is it a coincidence when two people meet briefly and then eighteen months later think of each other at the same time?*

*Was it a coincidence that my connection with Phil led to the magical facility where I offer dolphin retreats?* When we met at the Wesak

Festival, interacting with dolphins wasn't in my conscious awareness.

*Was it a series of synchronistic events that led me to the part of my destiny to work with dolphins?* What magnifies the likelihood that meeting Phil was part of my synchro destiny is that many of the entertainers and speakers I met at the festival contribute to my retreats.

What boggles my mind in a good way, is that this series of synchronous events was set into motion years prior to the wonderful opportunities that unfolded.

I invite you to take a moment and ponder what synchro destiny happenings have occurred and may well still be unfolding in your life. *What chain of connections has been set into motion as part of your synchro destiny?*

> Sometimes there are things that occur that defy words, experiences so incredible that your life is changed forever. A moment captured in time where you feel bliss and joy that you could only ever dare dream existed or was possible. It was such a moment when I first experienced swimming next to a non-captive dolphin.

Synchronicities often present themselves as validation for what you already intuitively know, such as feeling a departed loved one is nearby.

One day, I was writing about my deceased father and how he still communicates with me and our family from the other side. At precisely the moment I completed my story, not more than twenty feet away, a glorious eagle swooped right in front of my window.

> **"Synchronistic events offer us perceptions that may be useful in our psychological and spiritual growth and may reveal to us, through intuitive knowledge, that our lives have meaning."**
>
> **~ Jean Shinoda Bolen**

These little cosmic flags, that some call coincidences, are gentle taps on the shoulder from spirit inviting us to pay attention. When we place our awareness on what seems to be random coincidences, we may learn to welcome with a smile the way the universe divinely orchestrates our destined path.

> **We are given many signs by nature and its blessed beings. When we take the time to observe and take notice, we learn that there are many messages.**

By being consciously aware of synchronicities in your life, you become more in tune with the opportunities and choices presented to you.

## Story: Customer Service Counter

Megan was in a sporting goods store when "Dave Johnson, please come to the customer service counter" was announced over the intercom. Recognizing the name of a dear friend that she hasn't seen a long time, Megan headed for the service counter.

Dave Johnston walked into the store at the same moment, heard the announcement and headed for the service counter.

After warmly greeting each other, the two friends were surprised to learn that the person called to the service counter was a different Dave Johnson who worked in the store.

In the story, if Dave and/or Megan had been hoping to bump into each other, one or both of them might immediately recognize the situation as divine intervention. If neither of them had thought about the other for a long time, the serendipity of their connecting might not be immediately apparent to either one. However, as demonstrated in the story about how my meeting Phil at the Mount Shasta retreat, synchro destiny can take a while to unfold.

It is important that you don't dismiss an unexpected encounter with another as a mere coincidence. If you do, you could miss out on some of life's greatest gifts. You may not always understand why your path crossed with someone, but it may be that you are meant to connect for an important reason. That reason may not present itself right away, and instead will unfold as you are both ready.

If you are not sure why you have connected with someone, go within and ask Spirit why that person is showing up in your life.

There are many beings that are not of this physical realm and are ready to support you. But in order to receive their assistance, you must be open to accepting help. Whenever dealing with a situation where you are clear that you need help, ask for it, and be grateful when it comes your way.

Help may not always come from your own species, it may come from an animal, a bird or another blessed being of nature.

## Story: Crows

Over the years, I have learned that I am to slow down whenever a crow swoops in front of my car. Once when this happened, I slowed down and avoided what could have been a serious car accident. Another time, I avoided hitting a deer that suddenly bolted in front of my car. Although it isn't a regular happening, whenever a crow swoops in front of me while I'm driving, I slow down and trust that there's an unforeseen reason I'm being divinely guided.

It was a beautiful sunny day, and my son was at the wheel of his car as we enjoyed a leisurely country drive. Suddenly, a crow swooped down at the windshield. I glanced at the speedometer to see how fast my son was going. He was driving just over the speed limit. I decided that as he wasn't going dangerously fast, all would be okay. I didn't say anything. A second later, another crow almost hit the windshield. I turned to my son and said, "Maybe you should slow down a bit."

My son immediately let up on the gas as he glanced my way, and asked, "Why?" as we rounded a corner and spotted a radar trap. His brow shot up as he exclaimed, "How did you know?!"

I smiled and expressed a silent thank you to the crows.

**"There is no such thing as chance;**
**and what seem to us merest accident**
**springs from the deepest source of destiny."**
**Friedrich Schiller (1759 - 1805)**

## Nudges from Spirit

The divine gift of synchronicities are always at work in our daily lives. These little cosmic flags that may at first seem to be mere coincidences, are gentle taps on the shoulder from spirit inviting us to pay attention. They are especially prevalent in one's life during times of transformation, struggle or grief.

Think back to a time when you were processing a loss or transitioning through an unwanted change or challenge.

> Were there times when, seemingly out of nowhere, you heard or read words that gave you comfort?
>
> Did a song on the radio or television ever cause you to consider that a departed loved one was nearby?
>
> Have you ever noticed a scent that reminded you of someone you haven't seen in a while?

There are infinite ways the universe comforts and guides you. It may encourage you toward your intended destiny and away from that which will not serve you. It may provide you with comfort, so that you may move through a difficult time with ease and grace.

Although some signs from Spirit are blatantly obvious, others are less so. Sometimes, you may be led toward where you are meant to be at a given moment without the slightest inclination that you are being guided. Other times, you may sense that you are being directed somewhere but don't understand the *why* behind your inner knowings or a series of synchronicities.

Over the years, I have learned to pay close attention to even the most seemingly insignificant signs from Spirit. Doing so allowed me to be exactly where I needed to be when my mother suffered a stroke and needed my help. (Please see chapter seven, "Your Sixth Sense," for the complete story.)

Based on the Vedas, the sacred scriptures of India, Vedanta is one of the world's most ancient spiritual philosophies. When **Deepak Chopra** was asked about spiritual enlightenment, he said:

> **"According to Vedanta, there are only two symptoms of enlightenment, just two indications that a transformation is taking place within you toward a higher consciousness.**
>
> **The first symptom is that you stop worrying, things don't bother you anymore. You become light-hearted and full of joy.**
>
> **The second symptom is that you encounter more and more meaningful coincidences in your life, more and more synchronicities, and this accelerates to the point where you actually experience the miraculous."**

## Story: Synchronous Prescription

My mother was long overdue for new prescription glasses and especially new frames. She still wore the kind that had what I call wings off to the side. Time for an update! After much persuasion, she agreed to go with my sister and me, so we could help her pick out a new pair.

When Mom discussed buying new glasses with her optometrist, he told her that if she went to the eyewear store in a nearby mall, and mentioned his name to a clerk named John, she'd get a good discount. A great fan of a bargain, those were the magic words Mom needed to hear. Thrilled, my sister and I offered to take her shopping.

The plan was for Mom and me to meet up with my sister at lunchtime at her place of work. My sister was running a bit late, so while we waited for her, I asked Mom if she wanted to look at a few frames in the eyeglass shop next to where my sister worked. Mom adamantly responded, "No, my optometrist told me to go to the shop in the mall and ask for John and he would give me a discount." I assured her that she didn't have to buy anything and that looking at the glasses in the store might help her decide what style of frames she'd like. She reluctantly agreed.

While in the shop, Mom tried on a pair of glasses that looked fantastic on her. My sister arrived a few minutes later, and we both concurred that the frames suited her face and were extremely flattering. Mom's reaction was, "As much as these are very nice, I still want see John and get a discount." I suggested she approach the salesclerk and ask if he would give her a discount. Mom liked that idea.

Mom approached the clerk, told him she liked the glasses she'd tried on, but was planning to buy them at the nearby mall where a clerk named John would give her a good discount if she mentioned her optometrist's name. She then told him her optometrist's name.

The clerk replied, "Well, this is your lucky day! I'm the John your optometrist recommended. I work here now, and I will definitely give you a great discount."

## Story: Synchronous Reveal

What initially seems like the casual connection of two new acquaintances, could very well turn out to be an important aspect of both people's synchro destiny.

Sharon and Donna are two dear friends who met each other while at my home for a social gathering. As they chatted, Donna shared that she was going to a local college. Sharon responded, "Oh, I know someone who is also studying there," and mentioned his name. As they continued to talk, they discovered that unbeknownst to them, they were both currently dating this individual.

## Journey of Awakening

As a spiritual teacher and counselor, time and time again, I am asked two questions:

"What am I meant to do?"
"What is my purpose?"

As humans on our journey of awakening, we often seek life direction, but we do not "see" how synchronicities are continually unfolding to show us the way. We might fear the unknown, or know deep inside that a part of us is not ready to make a change or acknowledge a truth.

In our unconscious state of non-awareness, we search for logical explanations or brush off synchronous happenings as coincidences.

Sometimes, our ego leads us to believe that it knows best, keeping us trapped in our stories and false beliefs.

The answers you seek will present when you learn to trust your intuition and to allow, recognize and honor the synchronicities in your life. Then, and only then, will you enjoy and benefit from the infinite wisdom of the universe as a new and wondrous path filled with miracles unfolds before you.

Following is a recap of a wonderful story I read online. I tried to find out who the author was but couldn't. I was touched by the message and by the added synchronicity that followed my sharing this story with a friend.

## Story: God Works in Mysterious Ways

One Saturday night after working late, a pastor telephoned his wife to let her know he would soon be on his way home. It was about 10 p.m. He let the phone ring many times, but his wife didn't answer. A few minutes later, he tried calling her again. This time, she answered. When he asked why she hadn't answered the first time, she told him that the phone hadn't rung. Thinking that he must have dialed a wrong number, they let the matter drop.

The following Monday, the pastor received a call at the church office from a man who asked why someone from that number had called him on Saturday night around 10 p.m. At first, the pastor couldn't figure out what the man was talking about. But when the man said that the phone had rang and rang, the pastor remembered misdialing and apologized for disturbing the man.

The man said, "That's okay. Let me tell you a story. You see, I was planning to commit suicide on Saturday night, but before I did, I prayed, 'God, if you're there, and you don't want me to do this, give me a sign now.' At that point my phone started to ring. I looked at the caller ID, and it said, 'Almighty God.' I was afraid to answer."

The name of the church where the pastor worked was Almighty God Tabernacle, which explained why the caller ID on the man's phone read: "Almighty God."

On one of my road trips, while staying with a friend, I shared the above story. The very moment my story ended the phone rang. She had her system set up so that it would announce the caller. We heard: "Mother Teresa calling." We both looked at each other in total surprise and she started to laugh. That was the name of the school her daughter attended. The synchronicity and the timing were impeccable.

***Through daily observing and journaling,***
***you will soon discover the synchronicities leading you***
***toward your synchro destiny!***

## AWAKENING PROCESS

***Keep a Synchronicities Journal***

The vital first step to increase your recognition of synchronicities in your life is keeping a record of possible synchronous happenings. I cannot emphasize this enough.

Increasing your recognition of synchronicities isn't about walking around saying to yourself, "Hey, where are my synchronicities?" Rather, it involves trusting your intuitive knowings and the divine guidance of the *All That Is* while observing your unique view of the world (inner and outer) with an open heart and mind.

**Trust:** Keeping a Synchronicities Journal will raise your level of awareness, enhance your intuitive skills, and raise your level of trust in yourself and your purpose by increasing your trust of the divine force supporting you, every day and in every way.

**Allow:** You do not "look" for the synchronicities to occur; you *allow them to unfold.*

**Patterns:** If you diligently record your synchronicities over several months—no matter how insignificant a synchronicity or a coincidence may seem—you'll notice that one or more patterns emerge.

**Answers:** When reviewing your journal, you may find an answer to a newly formed question. You may even find an answer to a query that wasn't in your consciousness when you began to journal, but has been patiently waiting to be noticed.

**Comparison of Journals:** If you are keeping a daily reflection journal or diary where you write your thoughts and ponderings, by comparing entries in it with entries in your synchronicities journal, you may discover interesting parallels. Comparing the two may also allow you to recognize a synchro destiny event or a series of synchronicities guiding you along your path.

**Meditation:** To practice using your intuition to recognize a synchronicity, relax, and breathe deeply and slowly as you allow yourself to go into a meditative state. With a specific question or intention in mind, surrender all attachment to a specific outcome. Then let it go.

While you continue to meditate, place your awareness on images and messages that flow through your consciousness.

In the days that follow, place your awareness on obvious and metaphoric manifestations (clues, riddles and symbols) that may express themselves in response to your question or intention.

**Coincidences:** If your left-brain thinking determines that a coincidence has occurred, *trust* that it is a synchronicity.

**Be Ready:** Purchase several small notebooks and keep one with you at all times. Keep one in your purse or pocket, one in your car, one at your bedside, and one at your desk.

**Intention:** Each day, set an intention to be open to noticing any synchronicities, coincidences and unusual happenings.

**Daily Journaling:** Record at least three synchronicities every day. If your time is limited, feel free to keep what you write to a few words or sentences. Remember to include any emotional reactions to what you observed, heard or sensed.

***As time passes, you'll notice and be amazed by the number of synchronicities divinely guiding your life.***

**Specific Questions:** If you have a specific question, you might write it at the top of a journal page. Over the next while, allow and notice the obvious and metaphoric synchronicities that present. Be patient. It may take a series of synchronicities before the answer(s) you seek become apparent to you. As they often present as clues, riddles and symbols, some synchronous happenings may not appear to be related to your question. As the universe unfolds in mysterious ways, trust and record what you notice without judging the relevance to your query.

***Your noticing is your acknowledgement, and in doing so, you heightened your awareness.***

**Pay Attention:** You will receive messages in some of the most unlikely places. For instance, if you're wondering whether you should enter the healing field, and if so, what should you study, you might overhear someone mention Reiki. Within a day or two, while visiting a doctor's office, you might notice a pamphlet that discusses the many benefits of Reiki. Later in the week, you might see a promotion for a school that teaches Reiki.

**Review:** Wait at least one month to six weeks before you review the entries in your journal. Notice patterns, answers to questions you've asked, and synchro destiny encounters and happenings.

If you're about to embark on a new project, considering a career change, contemplating a move, or are in the midst of a transformation of any kind, notice what the universe is conveying to you through metamorphic and obvious synchronicities.

**Messages from the Other Side:** If someone you love has recently transitioned to the other side, observe the entries in your journal with an open mind to the idea that your loved one may be communicating with you through metaphoric symbols such as butterflies, ladybugs, coins, scents or rainbows.

# CH 7: Your Sixth Sense

Although some people are aware from a very young age that they have access to the *psychic energy* of the soul, the sixth sense, most do not. Yet, this keen intuitive ability is available to us all.

Those who tap into their psychic energy are commonly described as having extrasensory perception (ESP). According to the *Merriam-Webster Dictionary,* ESP is a "perception that involves awareness of information about events external to the self not gained through the (physical) senses and not deducible from previous experience."

As beings on earth, we are most familiar with our five physical senses: touch, taste, smell, sight and sound. But there is another unseen and subtle world around us that is the very essence of who we are. Yet, many of us have chosen the veil of illusion and forgotten the fundamental nature of our true being. It is time to awaken and develop our sixth sense!

Although you may have become numb to your innate sixth sense, within you remains an instinctive and superior cognitive sense that can be awakened, developed and cultivated. With practice, like tuning into your favorite radio or television station, you can tune into your sixth sense.

**By listening to your divine inner voice, your intuition, and by being keenly aware of synchronicities in your life, you will more easily discern the knowings and foresights available to you through psychic energy, your sixth sense.**

With spiritual practice, you can cultivate and enhance the empowering knowings and foresights of your sixth sense. At the forefront of psychic development is intuition. The second primary component is the ability to allow, recognize and interpret synchronicities with the aid of your intuition.

**Intuition:** When you silence the mind and listen, it is your inner knowings that will guide you toward opportunities, lead you to a life path that will bring you joy, give you insights on positive parenting, and more. Whatever it is that your heart desires, if you pay attention to the whispers of higher wisdom, your intuition, you are tapping into the psychic energy of the soul, your sixth sense.

**Synchronicities:** Synchronicities are the outer (physical) manifestation of intuition. Synchronous happenings are part of your sixth sense, and by recognizing them as they unfold in your life, you enhance your ability to predict future events, to stay out of harms way, to protect your loved ones, and to know what is a truth and what is not.

**Premonitions:** There are times when you may experience a premonition, a sense or a feeling that something is about to happen. This could be a good feeling; other times, it is as though something is "off' and you feel uneasy.

For some, premonitions can be unsettling, and especially unnerving when the presentiment is accurate, and even more unnerving when a correctly predicted happening is unwanted or tragic.

Whether you call it ESP, a sixth sense, or a sensitivity to premonitions, we all have the ability to sense future events. Out of fear, most people push this ability aside, ignoring what is a divine gift meant to protect and direct us.

When you step away from fear and cultivate this intuitive skill, you gain a deeper understanding of your divine inner wisdom, and realize that your sixth sense is a major asset and one of your greatest powers.

**Sixth Sense & the Sense of Smell:** The sense of smell is entwined with our daily experiences. Smells such as the scent of a favorite meal cooking, flowers, freshly cut grass, citrus fruits, perfume, and smoke often cause a full body memory of the experience associated with that particular scent.

When the source of a scent can be verified through one or more of our physical senses, the associated memory feels normal. This is not always the case when the presence of a scent has an undeterminable physical source. For those who have yet to realize that one's sixth sense can detect scents that emanate from a source that is undetectable via our physical senses, it is disturbing, maybe even frightening.

Scents are a common means of communication from beyond the veil. When you know this, smelling a departed loved one's perfume or favorite flower can be a comforting spiritual experience, and confirmation that love reaches beyond the physical dimension.

## Story: Can You Smell the Cigarette Smoke?

Shortly after my father passed, I often experienced a strong smell of cigarette smoke. Even though I tried, I wasn't able to determine the source of the distinct odor. Whenever I asked other people if they smelled smoke, their response was always the same: "No, what smoke?"

The times I smelled smoke became more frequent, and the scent was especially prevalent at night when I was nodding off, when I was alone in my vehicle, and during my facilitation of seminars. Whenever I felt stressed or in need of emotional support, the scent became more potent.

When I eventually shared what I was experiencing with my mother, she excitedly told me that she also frequently smelled cigarette smoke. A short while later, my sister confirmed that she often experienced the same phenomenon. After a brief discussion, the three of us agreed that as Dad was an avid smoker, the scent of smoke was his way of communicating with us.

One day, Mom asked, "Why does he have to communicate with us through the smell of smoke?" I responded, "Well, Mom, once you are on the other side, we will know you're close by when we smell lilacs."

During one of my *Communing with Dolphins* retreats in Hawaii, my sister and I planned a birthday celebration for Mom. As a surprise gift, we commissioned David, a talented artist, to create a painting of a magical moment our mother experienced when a dolphin brought her calf right next to Mom. It was as if this non-captive dolphin was letting Mom know how proud she was of her baby. It was a precious and tender moment that moved my mother to tears of joy and gratitude.

We celebrated Mom's birthday while enjoying another beautiful bright sunny day at our secluded retreat house by the ocean's edge. Mom, David and several other friends were relaxing on the lanai as my sister and I approached and were about to present the completed painting. Unexpectedly, we were overwhelmed by the intense smell of cigarette smoke. Only this time, everyone smelled it.

My sister and I looked at each other, smiled, and in unison, said, "Hi, Dad." Mom caught our eyes, smiled, and beamed in acknowledgment. In that moment, we knew that, typical for him, Dad was over the top with excitement at the anticipation of Mom receiving such a wonderful birthday gift—a gift that now had even deeper meaning.

**The sixth sense is the ability to delve into the subtle world, which is a realm of energetic and emotional information beyond the physical sphere. Using our sixth sense helps us perceive and understand relationships and events that transcend the way our intellect perceives situations.**

By using your subtle emotional and energetic senses, you may gain a greater perception of a world we cannot see with our physical eyes, such as beings that are no longer in the physical realm. You may also become sensitive to premonitions and be able to communicate with spirits, angels and guides on the other side, the eternal side.

Although some abilities are rarer than others, there are various ways by which one taps into the emotional and energetic senses. These include *clairvoyance* (clear seeing), *clairsentience* (clear sensations or feeling), *clairaudience* (clear hearing), *claircognizance* (clear knowing), *clairtangency* (clear touching), and *clairscent* (clear smelling).

As you continue your process of awakening, through spiritual practice, you can learn to cultivate, trust and act upon your psychic soul energy, your psychic intelligence.

## Sensory Abilities Descriptions

**Clairvoyance** (clear seeing) refers to visual psychic intelligence. You receive extrasensory impressions, symbols or mental images through your inner eye, also known as your third eye or your mind's eye. Clairvoyance transcends the limitations of time and space, and can see into the past, present and future.

**Clairaudience** (clear hearing) is when you perceive sounds, extra-sensory noise, words or music with your mind's ear. Often this can be hearing voices and receiving messages inside one's head and not with the physical ear.

**Clairsentience** (clear feeling or sensations) is when you feel other people's emotions such as their fears, anger and grief. You may also feel their emotional and physical pain. Empathetic and sensitive to others' emotions, a clairsentient person is often referred to as an *empath*.

As an empath, one is especially prone to becoming a "human sponge" as she/he may unconsciously absorb unwanted negative energy from those close by. At times, it may be difficult for an empath to be in a room filled with people. Clairsentients are excellent counselors and healers as they have an innate ability to understand their clients' emotions.

**Claircognizance** (clear knowing) is an inner knowing even when there isn't a rational explanation for why you know what you know. People with claircognizance ability may experience premonitions and/or forewarnings of things to come.

**Clairtangency** (clear touching) is the ability to perceive information about the owner of an object by touching or holding the item. This ability is also known as psychometry.

**Clairscent** (clear smelling) is the ability to perceive a scent without a determinable physical source or cause for the smell. Someone with clairscent ability can smell a scent associated with those on the other side; perhaps, a scent associated with a departed loved one such as cigarette smoke, perfume or the fragrance of a particular flower.

**Clairgustance** (clear tasting) is a rarer form of extra sensory perception (ESP). A person with clairgustance ability can perceive tasting the substance or essence of something from beyond the physical realm.

**Note:** All the above senses are heightened when one is in a higher state of consciousness, in an alpha state, a meditative state, or a joyful state.

**At times, intuition is your only voice of truth. When you learn to recognize, trust and distinguish your voice of intuition from the false voices of fear, doubt and indecision, you may literally save a life. When you act upon your intuitive knowings, the life you save may be your own or that of a loved one.**

The following true stories are examples of the instinctive and superior cognitive aspect of your sixth sense.

## Story: Can Intuition Save Lives?

It was a remarkable week. We had just completed an intensive eight-day mastery-level spiritual training retreat. The joy and transformations experienced by all were a huge confirmation that we were on the right path.

Late Saturday morning, while packing for my trip home, a powerful thought urged me to call the airline and book an earlier flight. As my current flight was booked for the next morning, I hesitated, decided it wasn't necessary to book an earlier flight, and continued packing.

The inner whisper became more urgent: "Book an earlier flight." This time I paid attention and called the airline and learned that changing my flight would cost $300. I decided to keep my original booking.

But no matter how I tried to ignore the intuitive nudge from the universe to book an earlier flight, the whispers would not silence. With the hope that the $300 I was about to spend would find its way back to me, I asked my assistant to drive me to the airport. The synchronous events that unfolded thereafter confirmed that the universe had heard my silent plea.

Several traffic detours rerouted us past and away from the airport.

When we finally reached our destination, I asked my assistant to wait in the car while I made certain that I could catch an earlier flight home. After confirming the amount of the additional fee, an airline representative offered to research other options. While he was doing so, the computer he was working on crashed. He apologized and assured me that it wouldn't take long to get the computer working again. Before the computer glitch was fixed, a staff shift change happened, and another clerk was assigned to work the counter.

Frustrated and uncertain as to how long it would take for the computer to be working, I decided to leave. As I was about to walk away, the same voice in my head said: "Wait! Don't leave!" I stayed put.

After several more minutes, the new clerk apologized for the delay, said that I'd waited long enough, and used another computer to book me on the next flight home, free of charge!

Traditionally, after retrieving my bags from the luggage carousel, I would telephone my mother to let her know that I'd arrived home safe and sound. Thanks to another computer glitch, there was a twenty-minute delay before the luggage from my flight was loaded onto the carousel. Once my bags arrived, I called my mother.
When she answered the phone, I said, "Hi, Mom!"

"Oh, how wonderful," she said, sounding cheerful. "You're home early."

"Yes, it is good to be home."

"Howrrr warrsshh yurrrr fffligghh?" she mumbled.

"Sorry, Mom, what did you say?"

"Howrrr warrsshh yurrrr...." She couldn't finish the question!

"Are you okay, Mom?" I asked, my mind racing as my heart pounded in my chest.

"Nooooo," she replied.

Realizing that Mom was having a stroke, I slowly and firmly said, "Mom, hang up. I'm going to call for help."

As he lived near to her, I telephoned my brother and he headed for Mom's place. By the time he arrived, she seemed okay, and had taken two aspirins, which the doctor later confirmed may have also saved her life. Although she didn't want to go to the hospital, we insisted that she go and were able to get her there.

Once at the hospital, tests confirmed Mom's blood pressure was extremely high and that she had experienced a Transient Ischemic Attack (TIA). More commonly known as a ministroke, left untreated, a TIA is often followed by a more serious, possibly deadly, stroke.

To this day, I remain grateful to God and the universe for the rather insistent nudges of the divine voice of my inner wisdom and the subsequent chain of synchronicities. These guided me to be there for my mother at the precise moment she needed me most. Mom might have passed away much sooner, maybe mere days after her TIA; instead, we had three more glorious years before my beloved mother passed from a massive stroke.

## Story: A Knowing that We Needed to Stay

The following is my recount of a true story that my dear friend Dennis shared with me.

Thirty years before Dennis had given any thought to the concept of intuition, he, his wife, and their one-year-old daughter were out of town visiting their friend Daniella and her family. After a great meal, the friends enjoyed a great conversation as they caught up with one another's lives and watched their children playing.

As the evening progressed, it became increasingly obvious that Daniella wasn't feeling well. Dennis's wife took him aside and suggested they leave so that Daniella could rest. Totally out of character for him, he refused to leave, saying he was enjoying himself. Under protest, his wife agreed to stay for a just a short while longer.

About ten minutes later, after visiting the bathroom, Daniella said that she didn't feel well and had passed blood. She then asked if Dennis and his wife would stay with their children so her husband could take her to the hospital.

It turned out that Daniella was in the early stages of pregnancy and had suffered a miscarriage. Later, when Dennis's wife asked how he knew that they needed to stay, he shrugged his shoulders.

According to Dennis, it wasn't until many years later when he learned about intuition that he realized he'd been guided by a nudge from his inner wisdom.

## Story: A Persistent Voice

Following is a true account of what happened to a woman named Saria.

Saria was standing outside a stationery and printing shop waiting for it to open. She'd only been there for a couple of minutes when she heard a loud and clear voice in her head: "Go to the thrift store."

Apparently, the store was about a block away, so she argued with the voice: "No, that doesn't make sense. I don't need anything from the thrift store. I have a tight schedule and need to pick up a few office supplies and get on with my day." The voice grew louder: "Go to the thrift store!"

She finally conceded and walked the block to the thrift store. About a minute later, someone came into the store and animatedly announced that a car had gone through a window of a shop up the street.

On her way back, as she approached the stationery and printing shop, Saria stopped mid-step. The vehicle that she'd heard about had crashed through the shop window at the exact spot where she'd been standing.

## Story: Formula One Driver Brakes Hard Without Knowing Why

The following story is a documented case study that was conducted by Dr. Gerard Hodgkinson, a professor at Leeds University near London, England. It involves a Formula One driver, and is a remarkable example of an instantaneous intuitive action at a nonconscious level. The result of this study was published in the *British Journal of Psychology*.

When nearing a hairpin corner, the Formula One driver hit the brakes hard. By doing so, he avoided smashing into the pile of cars that had crashed into one another on the track ahead. The driver had no idea why he had a sudden urge to hit the brakes hard. His quick action kept him from being harmed, maybe even saved his life.

The driver underwent a psychological forensic analysis, during which he was shown a video of the event. It was then that he realized that his cue to brake hard was that the crowd wasn't cheering him on, but was instead silently fixated on the track ahead of him. Although the driver hadn't consciously processed the danger, he sensed that something had happened and stopped his car.

Dr. Hodgkinson concluded that when both the "external world and internal world" are in perfect sync, our "brain is not only protecting us from danger but also calculating the absolute best path and decision to make."

## Story: The Nonconscious Intuitive Reaction that Saved My Precious Son's Life

When my son was about one-and-a-half years old, we visited a friend at her home. My son happily played with his toys in the living room as my friend and I sat at her dining room table and chatted over tea. My friend's house had an open layout, so I was able to watch my son. I could also see that the large area rug in the living room had a rather large bulge in the center, which I noted was a tripping hazard.

After my friend and I had enjoyed several cups of tea, without any apparent reason, my heart started to pound as the hair on my limbs stood straight and my entire body reacted as it would to an impending danger. I quickly glanced toward my son. He had the pointed end of a very large kitchen knife in his mouth! About fifteen feet away and walking towards us, with his next step, he was going to trip over the bulge in the carpet.

At super-human speed, I somehow managed to reach him, gingerly remove the knife from his mouth and then his hand. Images of the knife piercing my son's throat flashed through my mind. Horrified by what could have been, I went into shock.

My sudden and notable physical reaction to impending danger was due to my nonconscious intuitive mind realizing what my conscious mind had missed. Although I kept a close eye on him, without my noticing, my adventurous son had gone into the kitchen, climbed on a stepstool and retrieved the knife from the counter. No wonder parents end up with grey hair!

## Story: Blind Superhero

There are many stories we hear of superhuman feats such as a mother lifting a car off a child. One of my favorites is about Jim Sherman, a man blind from birth. Upon hearing his eighty-five-year-old neighbor's call for help, he ran through searing flames and somehow guided her out of her burning home. What was even more amazing, she too was blind.

## AWAKENING PROCESSES

***Developing Your Sixth Sense***

- Many of the processes in the previous chapters will help you to develop your sixth sense. If you have yet to read and practice earlier processes in this book, I invite you to do so as part of developing your sixth sense.

- A fun way to develop or enhance your sixth sense is by practicing kinesiology. In medical terms, kinesiology is the study of anatomy, physiology, and the mechanics of body movement.

  When used spiritually, kinesiology is a useful tool for cultivating your intuitiveness, your sixth sense.

  Process: While standing, relax and imagine that your body is like a pendulum. Decide in advance whether bending forward or backward will mean *yes* or *no,* and if bending sideways will mean something else, perhaps *maybe* or *ask again*.

  While still standing and imagining your body is like a pendulum, close your eyes, take a few slow deep breaths, and ask a question or set an intention that can be answered with yes, no, maybe or ask again.

  Continue taking slow deep breaths while being aware of the sway of your body and of any intuitive whispers from your soul.

Once you have determined the answer to your intention or question, if you want, ask another question or set another simply answered intention.

Following your kinesiology session, in a diary, record the answers to your questions and/or intentions, and any intuitive knowings that surfaced. As time unfolds, review what you wrote and determine how accurate your answers were. My guess is that you will be pleasantly surprised.

- Notice when you have a gut feeling about something. Strong feelings are an inner call to attention, and may be a premonition or a knowing about a forthcoming event or situation.
- Notice flashes of images in your mind's eye. Like gut feelings, they are an inner call to attention and may be a premonition.
- Keep a record of moments of déjà vu. Such moments could signal that you have tapped into a conscious stream from the past. Highly intuitive people frequently experience déjà vu.
- Practice *automatic writing,* which is allowing words to flow from your subconscious or from a higher realm of knowing. Intentionally allow your mind to step aside, relax, and tune into your higher self as you write whatever comes forth from your subconscious, or through you from a higher realm.

# CH 8: Are You Psychic?

**To be psychic is to *see* clearly.**
**The source of this ability is one's connection to Spirit.**

According to an article in Wikipedia, the word "psychic" is derived from the Greek word *psychikos* ("of the mind" or "mental"), and refers in part to the human mind or psyche.

The Greek word "psychikos" also means "soul." In Greek mythology, the maiden "Psykhe" was the deification of the human soul.

Unfortunately, the word psychic has been misused, and in some cases, has taken on a negative connotation. For some, the title evokes images of a person wearing gypsy attire as he or she peers into a crystal ball and spins tales of fortune and/or misfortune.

I do not refer to myself as being psychic; rather, I consider myself an intuitive. I *feel*, *hear*, *sense* and often *know* what is going on with an individual. I have cultivated this gift and am able to discern much information about a person and his or her life.

## Story: Resistance to Psychic Reading

Many years ago, when I first studied advanced clairvoyant training, I had no desire to do psychic readings. However, that soon changed, and I became fascinated by the process and especially interested in spirituality.

I now teach clairvoyant development, and many of my graduates are professional readers. During one of my six-month training programs, I had a group of thirty students. They were all informed that at the end of the program and before graduation, everyone was to bring a guest. Part of their curriculum was that they were all to perform at least one reading on someone else's guest.

Throughout the course, a student I'll refer to as Janet often expressed that she had no interest in doing the readings portion of the program. I could relate and smiled. On the day that everyone was supposed to bring a guest, she didn't. However, one of the other students brought two guests, one of which was coupled with Janet for a reading. Not surprisingly, Janet was not happy.

Once all readings were complete, we formed a circle in the center of the room, and guests were invited to provide their respective reader with feedback. A young man immediately stood and enthusiastically shared how profound and accurate Janet's reading was. He then looked at her and said, "I would like to book another reading with you."

When our guests left, Janet laughed and shared that she was sorry she'd resisted the idea of doing readings. Shortly thereafter, she became a professional reader.

**"If you want to make God laugh, tell Him your plans."**
**~ Woody Allen**

Being psychic does not mean you are supernatural. It is an innate gift, and some intuitives are more advanced or skilled than others. Just as one individual may sing, dance or play a particular sport better than others, psychics differ in their ability to "see" clearly. The good news is that through study and practice, one's intuition can be developed, refined and cultivated.

**Spirituality & Integrity:** To increase one's aptitude at a skill that emanates from Spirit, it's a given that a student is interested in spirituality and metaphysics. Students must also be openminded, value self-awareness, be nonjudgmental, have integrity, and trust that there is an accessible realm of divine wisdom. This is especially important for anyone wanting to become a professional reader.

**Professional Reader:** By accessing the realm of divine wisdom, a skilled reader can help his or her clients deal with life challenges, define and refine personal and business goals, gain clarity on issues, find inner strength, and feel supported by the universe. Acute intuition coupled with good communication skills allows a reader to understand clients' varied needs and to recognize, interpret and relay the voice of divine wisdom.

An individual may have a hunch or premonition about *something* or *someone* without fully understanding its meaning. A professional intuitive is better able to tune into his or her third eye (one's psychic center) and connect with Spirit and/or with spirit guides.

Skilled psychics/intuitives know when and how to ask for further guidance so they may receive a clearer image or a deeper understanding of what they are intuiting. They also know how to discern the information received, and relay it in a way that will be of service in guiding a client on his or her life path.

> **"Go inside and listen to your body, because your body will never lie to you. Your mind will play tricks, but the way you feel in your heart, in your guts, is the truth."**
> **~ Miguel Ruiz**

## Your Third Eye

One of the first steps in developing your psychic abilities is becoming aware of and activating your "third eye." Physically, one's third eye is the body's pineal gland, which is the *epicenter of inner vision.*

The pineal gland is considered to be the highest conduit of ethereal energy and is a connecting link between the physical and spiritual realms. In humans, the pineal gland is located directly behind one's physical eyes and near the center of the brain between the right and left hemispheres. It is cone shaped and about the size of a pea.

In addition to esoteric and mystical traditions, scientists, spiritual leaders and philosophers have long known the pineal gland to be the connecting link between your physical reality and the spiritual world. Sixteenth-century French philosopher, mathematician and scientist, **René Descartes**, referred to the third eye as "**the seat of the soul**" and the place in which all our thoughts are formed. Ancient Egyptians depicted the third eye in the **"Eye of Horus"** symbol.

Many teachings believe the pineal gland to be associated with the **sixth chakra,** which is also referred to as the third eye. When the sixth chakra center is *open*, one taps into their clairvoyant abilities to "see clearly."

**Chakras Explained:** Chakra is a Sanskrit word meaning *wheel* or *circle*. Chakras are conduits through which vital energy must pass in order to nourish and maintain physical, emotional, mental, and spiritual life as we know it to be. They are vortices of energy centers located in various focal points in our subtle body. When observed through the third eye, they look like spinning wheels of light and color that rotate opposite to each other, creating a spiral effect up the spine in a double helix effect.

**Free Booklet:** I invite you to download your free copy of my ***Journey Thru Chakras*** booklet. (www.Hannelore.ca)

Working in harmony with the hypothalamus gland, in response to electromagnetic energy, the pineal gland reacts like the neurotransmitter chemical *serotonin*. The interaction between the pineal gland and the hypothalamus heightens one's state of consciousness, acting somewhat like a light meter that magnifies inner visions.

The pineal gland is derived from what appears to be an actual third eye that develops early in the embryonic state but then later degenerates. Perhaps this may explain why children often sense future happenings and communicate with loved ones that have passed to the other side.

When activated through meditation and relaxation, the pineal gland or third eye is one's inner vision, the *observer*, that *sees* beyond the physical and views the greater picture of the *All That Is*. It is the link that develops your communication with, and understanding of, a higher level of existence.

**"The only real valuable thing is intuition. There is no logical way to the discovery of these elemental laws. There is only the way of intuition, which is helped by a feeling for the order lying behind the appearance."**

**~ Albert Einstein**

## My Preparation & Black Screen & Dot Experience

With my physical eyes closed, I prepare for each reading by bringing in my higher self and then ground and shield. Next, as I focus on my third eye, I ask my guides and beings of the highest vibration of light to assist me. I also tune into and connect with my client's higher self and ask for permission to receive information.

While looking through my third eye, my brow chakra, I tune into my heart. Most often, the information I receive flows through as a *knowing* or as *images flashing by one after the other*. But there are also times when all I "see" is a black screen and a dot. That's it! When I first started reading and the latter happened, I thought, "Great! What am I supposed to say to my client? 'Oh, I see a lot of black and a dot. Impressive, right?'"

With trust and patience, I learned that when I voiced a *creative* description of whatever I was "seeing," a more detailed image would unfold and have meaning. For instance, rather than say, "Oh, I see a black background and a dot," my creative description might be:

> "As I tune into your energy, all I am getting right now is a circle of light on the horizon. As I ask what this means and focus into it, it has taken on the form of a triangle. Now this triangle has taken shape and I'm looking at a pyramid."

At this point in a reading, an entire picture or story often unfolds. In the above true example, the person I was reading for was a priestess in a past life and worked in an Egyptian temple. During the reading, I received a very specific message that pertained to a current happening in her life.

**Historical Perspective:** Fear and ignorance, especially during the church-inspired thirteenth-century European inquisitions, led many people to view "seers" as devil worshippers and "healers" as witches or warlocks. Although it is difficult to determine an exact number, according to historians, tens of thousands (possibly millions) of innocent people were tortured and put to death.

As ridiculous as this rampant fearmongering was, the resulting fear has been passed on to subsequent generations through DNA. Without knowing why, it is quite possible that your subconscious mind will cause you to shy away from using your Spirit-emanating natural abilities to help others.

**To fully embrace one's intuitive gifts, fear must be transcended and released whether programmed into us by modern society, embedded in our DNA, or carried forward from a previous life or lives.**

**Modern-Day Fear:** In the late 1990s, I hosted a booth at a metaphysical trade show. Outside the building there was a small crowd of people blocking the stairs and holding up signs with fearful statements such as "The Devil Worships Here" and "Beware of Cults."

Although I was dismayed by this open display of fear, it saddened me that this ignorance still existed.

**Detecting Fakes:** Unfortunately, in our current time period, there are religious zealots, supposed spiritual teachers, purported healers and readers that misuse their power and take advantage of the innocent. *How then does one differentiate from who is genuine and who is false?*

As a person may seem very believable, it can take time and/or be difficult to detect when someone is not acting from a place of integrity. However, there could be subtle clues. For instance, you might have a feeling of not being safe or that something is off. You may feel like backing away from that person.

Should you wonder whether someone is being genuine, tune into where in your body you are feeling mistrust or doubt. Once you are aware of any associated physical sensations, trust that those feeling are your intuition guiding you.

Whenever I hear a spiritual teacher or healer make a statement that his or her way is the *only* way, or if someone claims to be the *only* teacher or healer I'll ever need, that is my cue to walk away.

**Heart-Centered Truth vs Fear:** It is natural for friends and family to be unnerved by changes they notice in you as you expand the horizon of your spiritual journey. There is no need to defend yourself or your gifts. Simply recognize that person's fear or doubts belong to him or her, not you.

**When another's fear penetrates your energy field, it is easy to misinterpret whose fear it was to begin with.**

There may be times you feel fear or anxiety, and it may not be readily apparent if it is your fear or if you have taken on someone else's. When this happens, pause, take a slow deep breath, and determine where in your body the fear feels strongest.

Next, as you tune into your heart center and without judgment, place your awareness on the part of your body feeling the fear and notice what thoughts come through. Ask whose voice it is that you hear. *Is it yours? Or does it belong to someone else?*

If it is not your voice, it is not your fear. With your intention, bless it and release it. With practice, you will learn to differentiate between your truth and the fears and illusions of others.

**The Power of Divine Wisdom:** We live in a time when it is safe to acknowledge, develop and express divine wisdom. As you develop your intuition and become skilled at accessing your higher self, you will feel a powerful personal connection with the divine. To embrace the true essence of who you are, it is important that you always come from a place of love.

## Notes About Being A Reader

**Everyone can learn how to conduct a psychic reading. It begins with trust and a belief in yourself.**

Although you may not realize it, you are reading others all the time. You may not understand how to interpret what you're intuitively sensing, and you may not always trust that your knowings are correct, but the fact remains that you are constantly reading others.

**Clouded Energies:** Sometimes your intuition and inner knowings are clouded by emotions and other energies. Other times, you may choose to analyze rather than trust your intuition. With practice and formal training, you can learn how to discern emotions from intuitive sensing, and thoughts from intuitive knowings.

**Counseling Abilities:** If friends and family often come to you for advice, you are likely great at clearly reading situations and people. It's also likely that you have excellent communications skills and are a natural counselor.

**Reading Blocks:** The person you are reading has the ability to block you from seeing or sensing something he or she doesn't want you to know, just as you might do if someone were to tune into you.

People put up blocks for numerous reasons. Some fear being judged by you. Others aren't ready to hear what you might have to share. Some clients are ashamed of something they've done or said. Some feel a need to hide intimate details about themselves.

When someone creates a block, consciously or unconsciously, it's likely that the information you intuit will be limited or nonexistent.

Should this happen during a reading, know that it is not a reflection of your abilities as a reader. Rather than doubt yourself, be honest. Tell the person you are reading that you're not receiving any information that might be of use, and then gently ask if he or she is open to receiving information. Most often you'll discover that the person is intentionally or unintentionally blocking the reading.

## Story: My First Reading as a Professional

In the early 1990s when I became a professional reader, I was unsure about how much to charge clients. Placing a minimal value on my worth and the worth of my services, I decided to charge a minimum amount. Although I was aware of the inherent challenges, my first professional reading was for a close friend.

When you are aware of numerous details about someone's life, there is a tendency to question information you already know that comes through during a reading. Sharing previously known information with a client who's also a friend can be unsettling. A reader may wonder whether it will invite skepticism about his or her abilities. After all, no one wants to be viewed as being inept, especially by a friend.

Prior to my reading with my friend, I prepared myself to receive information. Ignoring the butterflies in my stomach, I opened the reading session and tuned into her. Nothing came through. I tried to "see." Nothing. I tried to "hear." Nothing. I tried to "feel and sense." Nothing.

As the minutes ticked by, I thought to myself, "What am I doing here? Who do I think I am? How embarrassing. Well, obviously I am not going to charge for this!" If it were possible, I would have gladly opened a hole in the ground and crawled in.

After what seemed like an eternity of silence, my friend softly asked, "So, what are you getting, Hannelore?"

In full disclosure, I said, "I'm not getting anything. It's like you have this huge wall around you and nothing is coming through."

She replied, "Oh, that's because I put it there. I was worried about what you might get."

The wall instantly came down, and a flood of information came through, including a clear vision of my friend in a past life. She was walking with Christ. It was as if I were on a hill observing them walking along a narrow path. Accompanying my "seeing" was a "knowing" that they were talking about the *Essenes*, a mysterious brotherhood of men and women who lived before and during the time Christ was on earth.

When I shared what had come through, my friend said, "I have always been fascinated with the Essenes. But until today, I never understood why I want to know everything about them."

> **"I remember my first visit with my guru. He had shown that he read my mind. So, I looked at the grass and thought, 'My god, he's going to know all the things I don't want people to know.' I was really embarrassed. Then I looked up and he was looking directly at me with unconditional love."**
>
> **~ Ram Dass**

**Non-Judgment:** For many readers, and I include myself, intuitively received symbols and images sometimes don't make any logical sense. Over the years, I've learned to trust that although something doesn't make any sense to me, it may have meaning or will lead to information that will be valuable to my client. For me, it sometimes feels as though I really have to work for the information to come through, or "guess" what it might mean. (*Where do you think that a guess comes from*? It's your intuition.)

It is important to let go of any judgments about what you are seeing or sensing so that it does not get in the way of trusting and allowing your higher wisdom to come through.

## Story: The Singer

I was giving a reading for a new client. I didn't know anything about her, or why she came to me for a reading. When I closed my eyes to tune into her energy, the first image I saw was of a very strange female cartoon character with exaggerated features. Its mouth was wide open, and its tonsils were vibrating as though it was singing a long continuous note. I wasn't quite sure what to make of it, but the image persisted. It was quite humorous, and I thought, "What the heck is that all about?"

I went into trust, and at the risk of being totally off track, I opened my eyes, looked at my client, and asked, "Are you a singer? I get the sense that there is a song inside of you that wants to be heard and that you should be singing."

With that she exclaimed, "Oh, my God! That's why I am here. I want to know if I should consider singing professionally." The reading went on from there.

As an aside, this woman went on to record several CDs and enjoys a successful singing career.

## Benefits of Formal Classes

Some naysayers erroneously believe that if you have to take classes, you're not a natural reader and therefore not as good as someone else might be. Others are surprised that one's intuitive abilities can be cultivated. In truth, whether or not you're aware of your innate divine gifts, by learning new techniques and through practice your intuition can be enhanced.

**Self-Doubt:** One of the main benefits of cultivating one's intuitive abilities in a safe and controlled class environment is that you learn how to interpret, clarify and deliver the information you receive during a reading. Through exercises and feedback sessions, your intuitive knowings are validated, which diminishes doubts you may have about your abilities.

**Confidence & Trust:** Receiving positive feedback and validation increases your confidence in your abilities and gives you the courage to continue moving forward as a reader. Equally important, by developing your intuitiveness with the assistance of an experienced teacher, you will learn to let go of judgement and fear and *trust* your higher wisdom, your intuition. In turn, your increased self-confidence enhances your intuitive skills.

**Wisdom, Integrity & Compassion:** Through practice and from the feedback of your teacher and classmates, you'll learn how to clearly deliver the information you receive during an intuitive reading with wisdom, integrity and compassion—the three hallmarks of a sought-after reader.

**Readers are often blessed with many wondrous and miraculous insights. With clarity, a gift one occasionally receives is a connection with beings that are of a high vibration of light.**

**Cathy (Reader Insights):** "I had trouble with letting go of intellectualizing too. At the beginning of the reading, trusting my intuition was also a challenge. Consciously observing and letting thoughts come through without actually grabbing onto the thought was a new experience for me; but I did it! When a thought came through for a second or third time, I simply observed it again.

During my reading for Susan, a *thought* that she had lived on other worlds came through very strong and was followed by vivid images. I was hesitant to share what I believed was an intuition, not just a thought. Because of the images, I went for it. When Susan heard what I had to say, she got really excited and told me that other readers had told her the same thing. She now wants to learn more about her past lives on other worlds. It's kind of cool."

## AWAKENING PROCESS

***Locate Your Third Eye***

To find the location of your third eye, place the tip of a finger at the bridge of your nose, slide it upward between your brows to the slight indentation in the center of your forehead. Your third eye, also referred to as your brow or your sixth chakra, is directly behind the slight indentation in your forehead.

With your physical eyes closed and without straining, look upward and inward to the center of your forehead. If you force this process, you may experience an ache in your physical eyes or a tightness across your brow.

To help bring your focus to this area, wet your finger, place it on your third eye, and then remove your finger. The residual dampness on your third eye will help you focus your attention on this area. Alternatively (or additionally), you might gently tap your third eye several times with your finger.

Note: Locating your third eye is the first step in connecting with your *Universal Life Force Energy*, which we will cover in the next chapter.

## Higher Self, Silver Cord & Etheric Body

**Higher Self:** Your higher self is part of the divine collective consciousness and *knows* all that has ever happened, all that is happening, and all that has yet to happen. Once your conscious awareness is connected to your higher self, you can ask your higher self for guidance and answers.

**Silver Cord Lifeline:** Your higher self is your spirit/soul self that is eternal. It is connected to your heart via a silver cord, a thread that is your lifeline. When this lifetime is complete, the silver cord disconnects from your physical body as your body returns to earth and your eternal higher self becomes One with the *All That Is*.

**Your Etheric Body:** The etheric body is a twin of your physical body, and is actually a set of bodies that nest one within the other. The higher frequencies of the etheric body corresponds to the divine expression of universal love, compassion and wisdom.

The etheric body is also referred to as the *subtle* body, the *human energy field*, the *essence of the soul*, or the *aura*. It is bioplasmic and luminous in nature.

Although you cannot see it with your physical eyes, your etheric body surrounds and interpenetrates your physical body. Clairvoyants (clear seers) can view a person's etheric double.

## AWAKENING PROCESS

***Practice Connecting to Your Higher Self***

1. While sitting or standing, place both feet flat on the floor.

2. With your physical eyes closed, take a deep breath and imagine that directly in front of you is the most exquisite being of light, your higher self. Further envision that this being of light is connected to your physical heart by a silver cord, your life thread.

3. With your *imagination* and *intention*, use your etheric arms and reach out and gently embrace your higher self as you consciously allow it to merge with the cells of your physical body as you become one.

4. To help deepen the connection of your higher self with your physical self, take a deep breath and yawn. Yawning helps oxygen penetrate deeper into your body. This allows for "stuck" energies to be released.

Once your higher self is within your physical body, you may feel a slight shift that is as subtle as a gentle sigh.

## About Grounding

Grounding simply means to be connected to the earth while being present in the moment. If you are not grounded, you are not focused in the here and now. You are not fully present.

Becoming sidetracked, being in a rush, tripping over something, or not hearing what someone said are all indicators that you are not present in the moment. Animals and children are great teachers of the joy you can experience when grounded and present in the moment.

**Communication:** Being present allows you to be aware of what a person relays verbally and nonverbally, and is crucial for intuitive counselors. If you are not one-hundred percent present, your client will sense that you are drifting.

**Your Purpose:** You have an eternity to be in the Higher Realm, but a relatively short period of time to experience your physical body on earth. It is up to you to remember why you are here and what you are meant to do. Being grounded and present in the moment allows for clarity as you journey along your soul-intended path.

**I invite you to practice the grounding process on the next page.**

**Note:** When you complete the process, you will have brought yourself into the present moment. You may notice you are standing straighter and taller. Your body may feel lighter, and you may find it is easier to breathe. You may also notice you seem to see more clearly through your physical eyes.

## AWAKENING PROCESS

***Practice Grounding***

Note: If possible, do the following awakening practice with your bare feet on the earth.

1. With your eyes closed, breathe slowly and deeply.
2. Using your imagination, send cords from the bottom of your feet into the earth. Now, imagine these cords spreading like roots and becoming one with the earth's energy.
3. Next, imagine you are sending another cord from the base of your tailbone deep into the earth. Imagine this cord spreading like roots and becoming one with the earth's energy.
4. Allow the cords from your feet and tailbone to deepen until you feel a solid connection with the earth.
5. Imagine the energy of the earth is now coming up through the rooted cords and into your body. Feel the earth's continuous flow of energy travelling upward through your feet, your legs, your hips, abdomen, heart, throat, up through and out the top of your head.

Note: If you are holding onto any dense or negative energy, imagine it traveling through the grounding cords and into the earth as you release it from your mind, body and soul.

# CH 9: Energetic Boundaries, Shielding & Cords

The materials covered in this chapter will assist you in *awakening* and *aligning* with the Universal Life Force Energy. We'll also cover how to ground and connect with the earth's energy so that you will be fully conscious in your present-time power, and how to reinforce your protective personal shields of light.

## Awaken and Align with Universal Life Force Energy

Universal Life Force Energy is the all-encompassing divine energy of the *All That Is*. Known to every culture since recorded time, it is the vital force that gives and animates life. Much like individual water droplets in a body of water, Universal Life Force Energy flows within and around all things and connects us all as One.

Hawaiians or Polynesians may refer to it as *mana*. Taoists call it *qi* or *chi*. First Nations may refer to it as *Divine Spirit*, the *Creator* or the *Great Spirit*. The Japanese may call it *ki*, which is part of the word Reiki. In Egypt it is referred to as *Sekhem* and *Hai-Djerit*. Indian Yogi adepts may call it p*rana*. Christians refer to this energy as the *Holy Ghost*, the *Light*, or *God*.

Biochemists refer to this energy body as bio-plasma energy. Although it cannot be seen by one's physical eyes, bio-plasma energy within living cells can be measured and categorized into micro-frequencies.

**Other People's Energy:** We unconsciously reciprocate one another's energies. With practice and conscious awareness, you will learn to notice when you are feeling someone else's moods or emotions and are being influenced by their attitudes. The more you absorb and "match" others' energies, the more it affects your energy field. Once you fully comprehend how energy flows and how to work with it, you will be able to define what energy is yours and what is not.

We are often unaware that we are absorbing or matching another's energy. From time to time, you may want to pause and focus your awareness on what you are feeling in the moment, and discern whether you have absorbed someone else's energy.

If you become aware of dense emotions (fear, anger, grief, anxiety, panic) that you weren't feeling moments before, chances are you have taken those emotions on from the person you are with or have been thinking about. On the other hand, your energy may experience a boost when you are in the presence of someone who is filled with excitement and joy.

As a child, I was very empathic. I felt people's anger, and it frightened me. I felt people's fear and thought it was my own. I felt people's grief and it triggered mine. If I watched a movie, I cried tears of joy when there was a happy ending and tears of sorrow when it was sad. If someone emotionally shared a tale of woe, I cried right along with them.

When they were young, my kids teased me when I cried at movies or TV shows. As much as I tried to hide my tears, they'd peek over at me, laugh, and say, "There she goes again!"

Through my studies and journey of awakening, I learned to understand energy and have developed the tools that help me *not* to absorb others' emotions. As a result, I can remain strong and compassionate and effectively be of service.

If an intuitive counseling session, or any other situation becomes intense, and I find myself being pulled in by someone else's energy, I have learned to pull my energy back. Using my imagination, I fill and surround myself with a golden light. I call this ***going into gold.***

By *going into gold*, I can be there in support of my client without taking on or being affected by their "stuff."

This is a very simple, quick and effective method to no longer match and absorb another person's emotions and energy. Whether you completed a shielding exercise that day or not, as soon as you notice you are feeling someone else's emotions you are taking it on and into your body. The more you are inclined to do this, the more it affects your energy field. (See the "Practice Going into Gold" awakening process on the next page, and "My Quick Shielding Method" on page 198.)

We often do this and are unaware of it. As soon as you feel fear, anger or grief, or any emotion that just moments before you were not feeling, chances are you have taken on the emotion from the person you are physically with or talking with on the phone.

## AWAKENING PROCESS

***Practice Going into Gold***

By *going into gold*, you can still be there in support of your friend or an individual, but you are not being affected by their "stuff."

1. Take a deep breath, and imagine you are pulling *your* energy back from the individual.

2. Next, imagine their dense energy draining from your body into the earth. As it does so, it is cleansed, blessed and transmuted.

3. Now imagine you are being filled with a glorious bright golden light. Imagine this light expanding from your body and creating a golden shield of light around you.

4. Breathe into the gold, deeply and slowly.

## Creating Personal Energetic Boundaries with Shields of Light

In the past, I tended to take on other people's fear and/or be affected by their grief or anger. To help avoid doing this, I practice a shielding technique. This technique is done with *intention* and *love.* With conscious awareness, I align myself with Universal Life Force Energy, ground with the earth's energy so that I can feel my present-time power, and shield myself with light so as not to absorb another person's energy.

I refer to this process as: **Bring in Your Higher Self, Ground and Shield.** I consider this to be the most important technique I practice. I use it before I teach, speak, write, start an intuitive therapy session, make a major decision, attend an important meeting, or consult with professionals about my physical health.

With practice, you will become acquainted with the feeling you experience when your higher self is fully in your body. You will also learn to recognize when your higher self is not solidly in your body.

When I am shielded, I can still intuit, and to a degree, still feel and discern what is going on around me without taking on another person's energy. While my shield is surrounding me, I am not turning over my power. I am in control.

With *conscious intention,* I can allow this shield to soften and let my body feel some of the sensations I pick up from an individual. By softening my shield, I can determine what is going on for someone, and I am then able to offer my assistance. But as soon as another person's energy becomes too intense, I pull back and *fill* and *surround* myself with a golden light.

> **Protective shielding does not mean you are walking around with a thick dense armor of steel around you. Rather, you are surrounding yourself with shields of light, with the "force."**

You won't always have the time to go through the entire shielding process. There will be times when you have not shielded and someone who is chronically negative is suddenly within a few feet of you. Other times, someone will catch you off guard over the phone. By the time you have followed the steps to shield, they are already in your space.

## Story: Shielding & the Disheveled Woman

While still an apprentice, I assisted at a clairvoyant training workshop in New York. Newly taught in the art of shielding, I completed the exercise before my teacher and I went shopping in the city.

The two of us were on a busy sidewalk on our way to an exclusive jewelry shop in Manhattan when I felt and became aware of dense energy coming our way. The closer this energy came, the more agitated I felt as my body tensed in resistance. I recognized that it came from a disheveled-looking woman slowly walking toward us.

My teacher must have noticed what was happening for me because she asked, "Hannelore, did you shield?" Believing that the exercise I'd done earlier in the day was still protecting me, I replied that I had.

As the woman walked by us, I felt a sticky, disgusting energy attach and glom onto me. Even when this woman had walked well passed us, she kept coming into my thoughts as an icky heaviness weighed me down. As we reached the jewelry store and entered, I realized that I had to clear this energy out of my space as soon as possible.

In those days, security cameras were rare, but this upscale jewelry store was filled with them. As we rode up the escalator, I started the process of shielding and removing the energy with my physical hands. At that time, I was unaware that using my etheric hands would be just as effective.

There I was, waving my hands over my body and tossing this imaginary "stuff" into the ground when I realized I was in full view of the security cameras. I figured, *hey, I am in New York, I'm going to fit right in.*

I now understand when I feel resistance, even though I may have shielded earlier, that is my clue that I need to reinforce the shield.

**The awakening process at the end of this chapter outlines the steps involved.** I highly recommend you make this process a daily practice. As you grow familiar with the steps, you will develop a *quick method*, which will then only take a couple of minutes.

## My Quick Shielding Method

Having learned the importance of self-preservation when working with or around dense energy, I devised what I refer to as *the quick shield method*.

To quickly shield, I close my eyes for a fraction of a second, like a blink, and bring my awareness to my brow chakra (third eye) while also directing my attention into my heart.

I then silently say to myself, "SHIELD!"

My *intention* is that when I do this, all the steps I normally do in my longer shielding exercise instantly take place, thereby reinforcing my protective layers of light.

As an empath, I discovered that there are days and situations when I need to shield several times. When this happens, I often use the quick shield method.

**One of my favorite expressions is: "The Will of God takes no time...unless you believe it does."**

## Story: Huge Respect for Energy

When I was a young mother, we lived in an older home which required constant renovations. There were also a number of much-needed outdoor building projects, so I decided to take a woodworking class.

The course was fun, and over the next several months, I built a two-story Barbie dollhouse for my daughter, a captain's bed with a built in closet and a hidden chamber for my son, a glass inlaid coffee table, and cupboards around the washer and dryer. I also helped build a cedar tongue and groove deck around the swimming pool in our backyard. (When I'm excited about creating something, there's no stopping me.)

I acquired tremendous respect for tools, especially power tools. When not properly handled, they can be extremely dangerous. Just as it is commonsense to keep one's hands a safe distance from the turning blade of an electric saw, one must be mindful when working with varying degrees of energy.

When you protect yourself through grounding and shielding, you are less subject to other people's dense energy. Equally important, when you absorb negative or fearful energy, you could unwittingly pass that negativity or fear onto others.

Just as we can't see the air we breathe with our physical eyes, neither can we see energy. *Does this mean it does not exist? Do we have to "see" in order to believe?* It is human nature to want proof.

The following story is how I came to appreciate what can happen when one doesn't shield and protect oneself from negative energy.

## Story: Out of Control Fear

As we deepen our study of spirituality and cultivate our many gifts, there is an excitement in the recognition we have these abilities. While in class, I often hear students excitedly exclaim, "Oh, wow. This is real, I can do these things!"

For some students, realizing that their gifts of light are real, brings them to the realization that the heavy darkness may also be real. As fear takes control, some may experience headaches or become nauseous.

Still in my early years as an apprentice, I was assisting my teacher in an advanced clairvoyant training workshop. It was a powerful day with many *aha* moments. Most of the students experienced a deep connection with their intuitive gifts. As the excitement faded, several went into fear.

When I noticed one of the students holding her head and moaning, I employed a quick and powerful technique that instantly removes the energy that causes fear, stress or headaches. It involves a set of movements whereby I pull the dense energy from an individual, and carefully toss it into the core of the earth to be transmuted. Within a couple of minutes, the student said she felt much better and returned to her excitement and joy.

Upon seeing this, many of the other students asked if I could work on them. Before I realized what was happening, I had a long lineup of people wanting my help.

Instead of paying close attention to how I was performing this technique, in my desire to help, I inadvertently tossed each student's fearful energy into the area of my abdomen.

That evening as I was packing for my early morning flight to Vancouver, I became very weak and felt chilled to the bone. Hoping that a good night's sleep would help me feel better, I went to bed.

Still weak and freezing cold in the morning, I dragged myself out of bed and ran a bath. When I placed my hand under what should have been hot water coming out of the tap, it felt cold. It was as if there wasn't any hot water.
When my cab arrived, the driver took one look at me and asked if I was okay. At the airport, several people approached me and asked if I needed help. A concerned airline official took me to the lounge reserved for first class passengers so I could lie down.

Once my flight was airborne, I was moved to first class and given oxygen. While resting, I heard two concerned hostesses discussing whether they should ask the captain to do an emergency landing at a closer airport. My life essence was almost depleted.

When we landed in Vancouver, it took every ounce of energy that remained in my body to get home and to bed. It took several weeks for my body to fully recuperate.

This experience taught me to have tremendous regard for energy. I would not have experienced such an extreme reaction had I only worked on one or two people. I learned each person's energy has the potential to substantially impact another.

Whenever working with energy, my hope is that you'll learn from my experience and be diligent about staying consciously aware and respectful of energy.

## Understanding Cords

Cords are another aspect of energy, and there is a subtle difference between being "corded" in by someone and having their overall energy in your space. Both will affect your energy field.

To better understand how cords work, imagine a long extension cord, one end plugged into you and the other end plugged into a person focusing on you. This is not a physical cord, but rather an energetic cord carrying the frequency and vibration of the thought.

You do not have to be in the same room with someone to pick up the vibration of their thoughts, especially when those thoughts are directed at you. The person thinking about you could be on the opposite side of the world.

## How a Cord Affects You

Being aware of cord frequencies will help you determine whether something you are feeling belongs to you or someone else who may not be in physical proximity to you.

For example, let's say that you and I are dear friends. I'm travelling in another country, and one night I lose my wallet with all my identification, credit cards and money. It is late, and I have no place to stay. Unable to speak the local language, I am feeling alone and afraid and don't know what to do.

I start thinking about you and wishing I could talk to you. In that moment, without conscious intention, I sent a cord to you as I have "tuned" into you. This cord has a vibration of fear and that fear has to do with money and feeling lost. My fear thoughts travel through this cord, and in an instant, enters your energy field.

Meanwhile, you are having a great day at work, and for no apparent reason, you begin to feel apprehensive and uneasy. The more I keep thinking about you, the more uneasy you feel. The vibration of my fear matches the vibration of one of your fears, which becomes triggered in you. As this fear vibration enters your thoughts, it reminds you of your financial concerns, and you begin to process your fear thoughts around money.

At some point you may think of me and wonder how I am doing. We have now tuned into each other's frequency, like a number on the dial of a radio or TV station, only the channel is us!

**Cord Awareness:** The first step in recognizing that you are corded into another, is awareness. Notice if you are feeling a new sensation or emotion.

A telltale sign would be if you were feeling fine one moment, then suddenly became fearful or apprehensive and/or unexpectedly felt discomfort in your body. If this happens, take a moment, and tune into the place in your body you are feeling this emotion or discomfort. While focusing on that part of your body, notice what thoughts come in. As you notice your thoughts, ask who is speaking. This will help you determine whether the thoughts are yours or belong to someone else.

**Unintentional Cording:** We continuously and unintentionally cord into each other through our thoughts. Sometimes, a thought will be brief and lack significant energetic charge, and will simply fade away. Other times, it may be more intense and come from a place of fear, envy, anger, grief, or whatever the emotional energy is originating from the sender. This cord opens a channel between two people.

Often you are unaware there is a cord and the emotions you feel are not yours. When this happens, you may unwittingly act upon another person's negative thought vibrations, thinking it is your "stuff."

For example, the other person may be in a deep state of grief and going through depression. By thinking of you, they have unintentionally corded into you. You then feel their emotions, and as you are familiar with these feelings, you think they are resurfacing in you. This can then drain you, leaving you feeling depressed and lethargic.

**End of a Relationship & Cording:** When a close relationship with another person ends, often the cord between the two of you remains. At times, by simply thinking about that person, you become the sender of the cord. If you are the one going through a trauma, you may unintentionally weaken his or her energy. Until the cord is severed, you will continue to exchange your energies. However, removing the cord does not permanently end your relationship.

The following story is a personal experience that demonstrates what may happen when someone is "corded" into you.

## Story: Persistent Earache

A client of mine was dealing with major issues in her romantic relationship. There was a lot of verbal abuse and the situation was becoming increasingly volatile. During the session, we uncovered a connection between her current relationship and the physical and sexual abuse that occurred in her childhood. The session was transformative, and a tremendous amount of emotional healing occurred for my client.

The following day, I experienced a lot of discomfort in my ear that developed into a severe earache. I had earaches as a child, and they are not pleasant. The ache kept progressively getting worse throughout the day. I didn't have any painkillers and nothing I did seemed to help. Having heard somewhere that placing a clove of garlic in one's ear helps alleviate earaches, desperate to get rid of the pain, I tried it. FYI: It did not work.

Finally, after many hours, I received an intuitive nudge, a whisper from my soul that I was to follow my own advice. I stopped what I was doing, sat down in my meditation chair, closed my eyes, and did the exercise: **Bring in Your Higher Self, Ground and Shield.**

I then placed my awareness on my ear and tuned in to listen to my first thought. Instantaneously, I heard: "You need to hear my side of the story." On a *knowing* level, I knew it to be the voice of my client's partner.

Using my inner voice, I replied, "I will hear your side of the story, but you are not to be in my space." With my intention and imagination, I removed the cord that was in my ear and returned it to my client's partner. Next, I imagined that he was surrounded with light and turned him over to God. I then removed any residual energy from my ear and filled it with a healing light. Just like that, my earache was gone!

**I invite you to practice the three-step "Bring in Your Higher Self, Ground and Shield" awakening process that begins on the next page.**

## AWAKENING PROCESS

***Bring in Your Higher Self, Ground and Shield***

There are three main steps to this awakening process.

1. Connect with your higher self by aligning with Universal Life Force Energy.
2. Ground with the earth's energy so that you feel your present-time personal power.
3. Reinforce your personal protective shields of light.

As I mentioned earlier in this chapter, this exercise is one of the most important and basic techniques I use before I teach, speak, write, begin an intuitive session, or make a major decision.

**Note:** Connecting with your higher self and grounding were included with the awakening processes in the previous chapter. Some of the information is duplicated here.

I highly recommend this exercise become part of your daily practice and that you use it prior to making important decisions and when facing challenges.

At first, it may seem as though this exercise is a lengthy process. In fact, it takes very little time to complete. As you grow familiar with this process, you will develop your own *quick method* which will then only take a couple of minutes.

There will be times you may need to shield several times a day. As you become more aware, you will recognize when your body *contracts* and *resists* while in the presence of others. Occasionally, you won't have time to go through all these steps and will instead use your quick method.

**Suggestion:** While you are becoming familiar with this exercise, you may want to read this three-step process aloud and record it so you can listen to the exercise while connecting with yourself, grounding and shielding.

**Important Note:** If you have yet to practice the "**Locating Your Third Eye**" awareness process in the previous chapter, you may want to do so before doing this exercise.

## STEP ONE: Connect with Your Higher Self

Sit with your back straight, place your feet flat on the floor and your hands in your lap with your palms turned upward. Close your physical eyes and take several long, slow deep breaths. Breathe in deeply through your nose and out through your mouth.

Bring your awareness to your brow chakra, your sixth chakra, which is also known as your third eye. It is directly behind the small indentation in the center of your forehead. At the same time, bring your awareness to your heart, your fourth chakra where your soul resides. With *intention*, breathe into both of these areas.

Become aware of the feelings in your body. Notice where you may be holding tension, and breathe into that area. Each time you breathe in, relax and allow the vital Universal Life Force Energy to fill your body.

**As you continue to slowly breathe,**
**with each breath in,**
**focus on peaceful and loving thoughts.**
**With each breath out,**
**feel your tension and any other thoughts float away.**

Call upon your spirit guides and beings from the higher realm to support you with this process. With your imagination, allow your conscious awareness to acknowledge a shimmering radiant light directly in front of you. It is the most exquisite and beautiful being you can imagine. It is a body of light similar in size to your physical body. It radiates love, compassion and wisdom.

Allow your recognition to acknowledge that this body of light is your higher self and it is connected to you by a silver cord, a life thread.

With your intention and etheric arms, reach out and embrace your higher self and pull it into your physical body. Imagine it merging with all the cells, molecules and atoms in your physical body. You may want to imagine you are cocooned within a beautiful, translucent blanket of serene light as it completely fills your body with love.

Know that bringing in your higher self helps you see the greater picture of all that occurs in your life. To help deepen the connection of your higher self with your physical self, take a deep breath and yawn. Yawning helps oxygen penetrate deeper into your body where you may be experiencing "stuck" energies and allows for them to be released.

## STEP TWO: Ground with the Earth's Energy

While breathing slowly and deeply, use your *intention* and *imagination* as you send cords from the bottom of your feet into the earth. Further imagine these cords spreading like roots and becoming one with the earth's energy.

Now, imagine you are sending another cord from the base of your tailbone deep into the earth. Further imagine this cord spreading like roots and becoming one with the earth's energy.

With conscious intention, allow the cords from your feet and tailbone to deepen until you feel a solid connection with the earth. If you don't feel, sense or "see" this happening, trust that it is so.

With each breath or yawn, imagine that the energy of the earth is now coming up through the rooted cords and into your body. Feel the earth's continuous flow of energy travelling upward through your feet, your legs, your hips, abdomen, heart, throat, and up and out the top of your head.

Take a deep breath and imagine that, like a fountain of infinite energy and light, some of this earth energy is now branching out and flowing down and across your shoulders, down your arms and out your hands as it continues to bathe you in cascading layers of light.

### STEP THREE: Reinforce Your Personal Protective Shields of Light

Imagine Universal Life Force Energy as a translucent white or golden light coming down from the universe and into your crown chakra at the top of your head. Allow this continuous flow of energy to travel down the back of your spine, down your legs, out through your feet and into the earth where it will mix with the earth's energy.

You might *see* this flow of energy as a color, or you may *feel* the energy. Either way, allow yourself to "trust" that this is happening. Know that with each breath out, you are releasing excess energy and any dense thoughts and emotions. Imagine these draining down and out the cords to be transmuted in the earth.

Bring your awareness to how the earth and Universal Life Force Energy meet in your heart and expand, filling every cell and molecule with divine translucent white or golden light. With intention and trust, imagine this light now expanding as it creates a "shield" of light and love. *This is your first shield of light.*

Visualize a spiral of light now surrounding your first shield of light as it creates a *second shield of light.*

Imagine several other continuous spirals of light surrounding you *and* the first two shields of light as they create your third shield, then your fourth, fifth, sixth and seventh shields of light.

Take several more slow, deep breaths. When you are ready, open your eyes.

Finally, if you like, wrap your arms around yourself and give yourself a hug!

***So Be It and So It Is***

**Note:** In this awakening process, we have used seven shields of light as they relate to the seven major chakras, which are explained in the ***Journey Thru Chakras*** booklet. To download your free copy, visit www.Hannelore.ca

# CH 10: Spirit & Physical Guides

We all have many forms of spirit and physical guides.

**Physical Guides:** Our physical guides nurture and support us. These are people we feel safe to confide in and who encourage us to be the best we can be. A physical guide may be a parent, a sibling, a grandparent, a close friend, a significant other, a teacher, or a counselor, to name just a few.

**Inner Guides:** We also have many inner guides who are our allies. They boost our self-esteem and help us make good decisions. A few of these include the inner parent, inner adult, inner teacher, inner friend, inner artist, inner critic, inner healer, and most importantly, the *inner child.*

**Inner Child Guide:** Your inner child is the aspect of you that influences all the other inner guides. Your inner child is your innocence and inspires your childlike wonder. This is the pure essence of you. She or he teaches and reminds you to play and that you need to be loved and nurtured. She or he also encourages you to stay present and connected with the earth.

Your inner child controls your emotions. If you were emotionally wounded as a child, these hurt emotions may still be stored within you, and your inner child will act them out. If you overreact or behave like a child when something doesn't go your way, that is likely your inner child expressing itself. Your inner child is also at the forefront when you experience resistance or fear when trying something new.

## AWAKENING PROCESS

***Practice Communicating with Your Inner Child***

Your inner child resides in your heart. I encourage you to tune in with your inner child by following the process below.

1. Close your eyes, take several slow deep breaths and ground.

2. Place your hand on your heart and bring your awareness to this area as you telepathically acknowledge your inner child. Choose words that feel right to you. For instance, you might say, "Hi, me," or "Hi, there," or "I love you."

3. Continue communicating with your inner child. For example, below are a few questions you might ask her or him.

"Are you okay?"
"What is going on for you?
"Is there anything you want me to know?"
"What fun activity would you like to do today?"

Be sure to listen to what your inner child has to share with you. You might also respond to what you hear, and again listen for what is truly being said.

**Be Reassuring:** Your inner child might respond in ways that let you know that she or he needs reassuring or encouragement. When this happens, you may respond with comments like the ones below.

"I hear what you're saying."
"What can I do to help?"
"Would you like a hug?"
"What do you need to feel safe today?"

**Note:** If you find that you cannot immediately connect with your inner child, don't give up. She or he may be hiding and need time to trust and come forward.

**Triggered Memories:** The more you lovingly communicate with your inner child, the more at peace you feel. However, if communicating with your inner child triggers a powerful and painful memory that you cannot come to terms with on your own, you might consider consulting with a therapist or counselor you trust.

**The more you openly and lovingly communicate with your inner child, the more in touch you are with your true inner self.**

## More About Spirt & Physical Guides

**Nature Spirits:** These guides are devas that often guide you with your connection to the wonders of nature. They may even regulate how your garden grows. Some refer to nature spirits as elves, gnomes or fairies.

**Higher Self Guide:** One's higher self is the divine guide that is One with the *All That Is*. It offers you wisdom, discernment, understanding, and knowing. This guide has the collective memory of your past lives, helps you see the greater picture of your present life, and knows your future probabilities.

**Spirit Guides**: Spirit guides are non-physical, disembodied entities that support you and serve as a protector and a guide. They may assist you during difficult times, help you learn lessons, lead you to your intended path, and keep you safe.

They may sometimes be referred to as guardian angels. In Native American teachings, they can be in the form of totems, which are spirit beings. They can also be in the form of animals, often referred to as power animals.

**Below are a few subtle and not so subtle ways to recognize when a spirit guide is in your presence.**

**Numbers:** A sign that brings one's awareness to the possibility that a spirit guide is present is being drawn to repetitive numbers. For example, noticing 11:11 or 3:33 or 12:12 on a clock. You may notice meaningful repetitive numbers in other places. For instance, 777 or

888 on license plates or street addresses. When the same repeated numbers continually present in your life, there is a high likelihood that one or more spirit guides are communicating with you.

In my dear friend Joy's family, whenever a family member notices repeated numbers on a clock, especially 11:11, that person announces the time followed by "make a wish, the angels are listening."

When the same friend was going through a rough time, she asked her spirit guides for a sign that things would change for the better. A few minutes later, she took a friend's dog for a walk in the schoolyard next to where they lived. As they reached the center of the park, she spotted a nickel glistening in the sunshine. As the number five signifies change, she knew that her life was about to take a positive turn, which it did almost immediately.

**My Departed Loved Ones:** There have been many signs in my life that some of my departed loved ones are guiding me from the other side.

As I wrote in chapter seven about one's sixth sense, the smell of cigarette smoke without a determinable source is a sign that my father is present. Once while teaching a class, I suddenly saw an image in my mind's eye of my departed Uncle Joe. The huge smile on his face gave me a feeling of being on the right track with what I was sharing.

While dining with colleagues, I spoke of a very dear childhood friend, Rosel. I hadn't thought about her in years, and was surprised when I suddenly burst into tears. When my family moved back to Germany for a year when I was ten, Rosel and I became the best of friends. A hard-plastic doll she gave me, now an antique, is displayed in my china cabinet.

Over the years, we lost touch. Sadly, she died at a young age. My unexpected and strong reaction as I mentioned her name let me know that she was close by.

**Animal Guides:** Birds, insects and animals often guide us or give us messages. For me, as I shared in chapter six about synchronicities, when a crow swoops in front of the windshield while I'm driving, I know it's cautioning me to slow down. In the same chapter, I wrote about the validation given to me when an eagle flew directly in front of my window upon my completing a story. That felt like an exclamation mark!

**Following are a few stories that may help you recognize when your spirit guides are reaching out to you.**

## Story: My Mom & the Ladybugs

From the moment my mother passed, ladybugs have been a significant and often noted sign of her presence. Connecting with her brings me joy, especially when I feel her encouraging me to continue writing.

Nearing the completion of the *Your Soul's Whispers Trilogy*, I spent the last couple of weeks writing outdoors while sitting at my patio table. As I finished the last chapter, with a feeling of satisfaction and accomplishment, I took a deep breath, stretched my arms above my head, and looked up. There above my head on the patio umbrella was a ladybug. I felt a warmness envelop me. It was as though my mother was standing before me and smiling,

## Story: Songs Letting Me Know Mom was Nearby

I enjoy listening to quiet and peaceful music while writing, so I often have the television tuned to the channel with soothing spa music. Not too long ago, I walked by and glanced at the TV as the screen displayed the origin of the piece of music playing. I was surprised the piece was from my mother's birthplace, a very remote village in Germany. The very next song was "Ava Maria," my mother's favorite song.

**Although we may not always notice them,<br>signs such as those I've received from departed loved ones<br>are meant to let you know you are not alone.**

## Story: Rainbows of Love

A dear friend of mine loves to share this story: Whenever her elderly father faced health challenges, she would see a rainbow and know he would be okay.

Her sister called to tell her that their dad was going to have a lung biopsy. The next day while driving, she saw a rainbow in a field. After accompanying her father for a prostate biopsy, the two of them saw a rainbow.

While watering the garden on a beautiful summer evening, her sister called to let her know that their dad had been scheduled for an operation to clear the plaque from his carotid artery. "Oh, oh," she thought. "The skies are clear, the air is dry and hot, and there is no rain in the forecast. How am I going to see a rainbow?" As she turned the hose back on to continue watering the garden, a rainbow of colors appeared in the mist.

When her dad passed away a few years later, as the two of them had often talked about the rainbows that had appeared to let her know he'd be okay, my friend looked for rainbows in the sky, hoping that he'd send a few to let her know he was doing well.

A year and a half passed, and she still had not seen a single rainbow. It wasn't until she was driving through Northern Ontario that she discovered the reason for the absence of rainbows in her life.

When her dad was nearing the end of his life, he asked my friend if she thought he'd ever return to his favorite natural spring in Northern Ontario, which he called "pond twenty-seven." She responded, "Of course! If you want to return to pond twenty-seven, then you will!"

As she drove along Highway 11 on her way to North Bay, Ontario, brilliantly displayed above a forest area was the most beautiful rainbow she'd ever seen. Her father had returned to his favorite place.

## STORY: Rosalyn, You Are Really *Out There*

I was watching TV, putting off completing a challenging assignment for my second-year interfaith minister studies. The assignment was to complete a minister's manual for use while officiating events. One ceremony remained.

My very dear friend Rosalyn had just unexpectedly passed away, and I was feeling the pain of losing her. Her family asked me to perform her ceremony and deliver her eulogy, which I had yet to prepare for. Coincidentally, the ceremony I had yet to complete for my course was performing services and celebrations of life.

I was happily procrastinating, when the TV channel changed. As the remote control was sitting on the coffee table, I knew that I hadn't accidentally changed the channel. Thinking that one of my cats might have stepped on the remote, I glanced at the coffee table. Nope! The cats were elsewhere.

I picked up the remote, changed the channel back to the show I was watching, and returned the remote to the coffee table. A moment later, the channel switched again. Determined to finish watching my show, I again switched back to the channel I was watching. A second later, the television turned off.

Images of my supportive and loving friend flashed in my mind's eye, as I thought, "Okay, Rosalyn, I get it!" I immediately started writing her eulogy, sometimes through tears and other times through laughter, as I reminisced about our times together.

That night, as part of my before-bed ritual and meditation, I cozied up in a lounge chair on the balcony and gazed up at the sky. It was a clear night with especially bright stars. After several minutes and a prayer of gratitude, I thought, "Rosalyn, I know you are really out there, but it would be great if you could give me some kind of sign...."

Before I could complete my thought, a falling star appeared. Instead of shooting diagonally across the sky as shooting stars normally do, this star slowly dropped downward in a straight line.

A few minutes after the star faded, I thought, "Thank you, Rosalyn. That was a great sign, but it would be really terrific if you could show me absolute proof that you still...." Again, before I completed my thought, a star I'd noticed grew larger and larger until it was as bright and big as a full moon, then it slowly shrunk in size until it disappeared.

Awestruck, but still hoping for more, I thought, "Wow, Rosalyn. I appreciate that those were spectacular signs, and I thank you. But in full disclosure, I was hoping to see your Spirit, your essence standing before me." Although I waited with anticipation that my dear friend might suddenly appear before me, she didn't.

While performing Rosalyn's service, I recounted my experiences with the stars. Her children and family members were profoundly grateful. Those were the messages they needed to hear to bring them solace.

Although I regularly spend time stargazing, I never again witnessed anything as wonderful as I did that night. Thank you, Rosalyn!

## CH 11: Your Current & Desired Legacies

A legacy may be material possessions left behind for others to enjoy. These could be family heirlooms such as a great grandparent's watch or necklace, a piece of art or a musical instrument. A legacy can be a beautiful home that has been tenderly cared for or it can be a piece of land that has been in the family for generations. It could be an embedded commemorative plaque on a wall, or dedicated park bench.

A legacy can also be mementos such as a song or a poem written from one's heart, a book, or a collection of favorite family recipes. These are all wonderful legacies.

Equally important, a legacy is the culmination of the qualities and accomplishments a person has attained. It is the story of one's life so they may be remembered.

I am reminded of a quote from the movie *Stand Up Guys.* Al Pacino's character said, "They say we die twice. Once when the breath leaves our body, and once when the last person we know says our name."

**Your legacy serves as a guide to support and influence others in their life choices.**

A written legacy may include stories about your travels, artistic endeavors, selfless actions, values, inspiring parables, life wisdom, your dreams and successes. It may also include your disappointments and what you did to overcome challenges.

As I was writing this chapter,
it dawned on me that this book is part of my legacy.

**I invite you to write your legacy.**

The first part of this chapter, "**Writing Your Current Legacy**," is meant to encourage you to unveil and share what you have learned thus far on your soul-intended path.

The second part, "**Writing Your Desired Legacy**," is meant to further awaken your dreams as you listen to the whispers of your soul and continue to reach for all you wish to be and do in this lifetime.

**"Don't Die with Your Music Still in You."**

**~ Dr. Wayne Dyer**

> **"Death is not the biggest fear we have; our biggest fear is taking the risk to be alive – the risk to be alive and express what we really are."**
>
> **~ Miguel Ruiz**

## Writing Your Current Legacy

Have you ever wished that you'd known a relative who walked this beautiful earth before your time? Perhaps you have wondered about your great-great-grandparents or a great uncle or aunt that was such a character people still smile whenever his or her name is mentioned? Imagine what a gift it would be if you were able to read an account of that relative's innermost thoughts, dreams, accomplishments, challenges, beliefs and insights.

With the above in mind, I invite you to find a special journal and write your legacy, perhaps for your children or grandchildren. Such a gift is bound to become a cherished family heirloom that will be passed on to subsequent generations.

If you're so inclined, you may want to publish your legacy so that people other than family members can learn from and be inspired by your prose.

Inherent in every dream, struggle, mistake, accomplishment, and regret are hidden blessings and wisdom from which others can benefit. Writing about some events, people and experiences may bring a smile to your face, others may bring you to tears.

You may discover that writing your legacy becomes a powerful life-changing process. Revisiting your legacy from time to time may provide you with wonderful insights about who you are as a person.

One of the most empowering aspects of writing your legacy is that you will see your life and self more clearly. Having defined who you are, you may decide to make changes in your life as you move toward a vision of who you could be. You may even adjust your beliefs and priorities.

**"I would like my life to be a statement of love and compassion – and where it isn't, that's where my work lies."**

**~ Ram Dass**

## AWAKENING PROCESS

***Write Your Current Legacy***

Below are a few points and questions meant to spark your ponderings as you consider what you might want to write about in your legacy journal. Not all are meant to be answered, rather they are simply meant to inspire you.

- Go back through the pages of your life and remember a time when you experienced tremendous joy, or a moment when you felt overwhelming love and gratitude.

- Think of the times you truly desired something in your life. You wanted it so bad you could almost taste it. You just knew you were going to make it happen, and you did. *How did it come about? Did a check come out of nowhere? Did a friend offer help? What action did you take to make it happen?*

- Now think of a time you truly desired something, but you let fear get in the way, be it your own or someone else's. What insights did you gain? Do you have regrets?

- Have you ever been bullied, and if so, how did you get through this experience?

- What were your greatest accomplishments and how did you attain these?

- Of all of the emotions you have experienced, which one was the most powerful and why did it impact you?
- If you are a parent, what are the do's and don'ts you have come to know about raising children?
- Have you climbed an actual or proverbial mountain and experienced the view from the top? What did you come to know?
- What lessons or wisdom granted to you by an elder proved to be the most helpful in your life?
- Have you overcome a personality trait such as shyness? If so, did taking a course, reading a book, or the wisdom that comes from age help you?
- What have you come to know that you wish you had known when you were younger?
- What were your greatest challenges and disappoint-ment's and how did you transcend these?
- What are the most important pieces of information you have come to know about failure or success?
- Do you have any insights on how to mend a broken heart or overcome deep sadness?

## Writing Your Desired Legacy

**If you imagine your heartfelt desire as a sweet and harmonious song, the voice you hear singing may be the whispers of your soul celebrating.**

Writing your current legacy may have led you to adjust your priorities, perhaps by awakening your desire to revisit dormant dreams, goals or ambitions.

**What is it that you desire?**

As with any desire, when you shift your state to believing that it is possible, followed with an enthusiastic action plan, it will absolutely and undoubtedly occur.

**To *desire* is a creative vibration greater than a *want.* It often comes from the heart. The attainment of a desire often brings peace of mind, happiness and emotional satisfaction.**

**Imagination:** Imagination is the foundation of creation. It plants the seed to bring into your life that which you desire.

**Intention:** A desired legacy is written by a *future you*. Use your *imagination* and *intention* and *trust* that your dream or goal has already been manifested by the universe and is waiting for your belief to match its vibration.

**Belief:** When you believe with all your heart that it is doable, you will attain what your heart desires. It's really that simple.

**Clarify:** Begin with clarifying what you desire. Once clear, imagine the *future you* has experienced and lived these desires. An example may be to consider all the places you would like to travel, and then imagine the *future you* has already visited all these places.

**The story of your life is your legacy you are writing every day.**

**"Legacy is not leaving something for people.**
**It is leaving something in people.**
**~Peter Stople**

## AWAKENING PROCESS

***Write Your Desired Legacy***

Spend a few precious moments each day to pause and breathe deeply into your heart. Place a hand and your awareness on your heart center and ask, "What is my ultimate desired legacy?" (Feel free to use whatever words resonate with you.)

Listen to the whispers of your soul. Write whatever inspirations come forward. As you allow your imagination to focus on your desired legacy, allow it to grow.

Imagine that in this moment you are the perfect image of who you aspire to be.

Imagine you are making a positive and impactful difference in this world. How are you doing this?

Imagine you could *be*, *do*, and *have* anything you desire.

Where would you live?
Where would you travel?
What type of work and/or service would you offer?
What gifts of wisdom would you like to leave behind?
What are your values?
What are your hopes and dreams?
Who would you be with?

**Let your imagination soar!**

May the following poem inspire you as it continues to inspire me.

### You Can Be Whatever You Want to Be

"There is inside you,
all of the potential to be whatever you want to be.
All of the energy to do whatever you want to do.
Imagine yourself as you would like to be,
doing what you want to do,
And each day, take one step
towards your dream.
And though at times it may seem too
difficult to continue,
hold on to your dream.
One morning you will awake to find
that you are the person
you dreamed of.
Doing what you wanted to do
simply because you had the courage
to believe in your potential
and to hold on to your dream."

**~ Donna Levine**

## With Gratitude

**Is there something tugging at your heart,**
**a whisper from your soul that says...**

***"Live your purpose before it's too late.***
***You are here for much greater, grander things than this!"***

Dear reader, new and longtime friends,

With deep gratitude and love, I thank you for allowing me to share my journey and insights with you.

I invite you to step into your courage, and break through illusions and imagined barriers to rise into a new level of consciousness.

The power is within you to BE all that you dare to dream. You are the change you wish to see. Be open to the infinite possibilities within your awakening.

Individually and together as One, may we consciously enter the "Unified Field" with infinite love, compassion, peace, and wisdom.

May we be the beacon of light so that others may see their way through the darkness.

***Our time is now!***

***We are the ones we have been waiting for!***

*May the blessings of light
and love be upon you.*

*Light is the message and the
blessings from Source.*

*Your heart is pure love
and pure love is pure light.*

*May the light shining within you
remind you of the
beauty of creation that you are.*

*As you let your light shine,
allow it to radiate from your heart
and through your eyes.*

*Share it with others, so that they may
see their way through the darkness
returning to the light of home.*

*You are an important part of Source's plan.
Your divinity is a blessing to this planet.*

*May Source's light and angels always
watch over you and keep you safe.*

*So Be It and So It Is*

*Infinite Blessings, Hannelore*

## About Hannelore

Through another's eyes, Hannelore exudes poise, wisdom, grace, compassion, and love. Through Hannelore's eyes, she is a grateful vessel for the abundant and unwavering love of the All That Is.

Hannelore (her birth name meaning "with the grace of God") was born in Bavaria, Germany. When she was three, she and her family moved to a remote coastal community in British Columbia, and then to Vancouver, B.C., where she currently resides.

Gregarious and adventuresome, in her late teens and early twenties, she enjoyed a successful career as an actress and model. A number of years later, after obtaining a degree in marketing, she founded Sky High Agencies Inc. and contracted with television commercial, music, and animation production companies. At the height of her business career, she represented over fifty well-known Canadian and American television commercial directors and cinematographers in fourteen major cities throughout the U.S. and Canada.

After recovering from a car accident and a massive head injury in the mid-nineties, Hannelore's priorities somersaulted and grounded her firmly on her spiritual path. For over twenty years, she has facilitated magical life-transforming retreats for individuals and couples, some of which take place in Hawaii where participants respectfully commune with non-captive dolphins.

After studying comparative religions and dimensions of psychology with The New Seminary, Hannelore was ordained as an interfaith minister at the Cathedral of St. John the Divine located in New York City. She is a Reiki master, studied and teaches shamanism, and is a graduate of numerous certified counseling and metaphysical courses. Some of her training includes the Medicine and Mystery School, advanced clairvoyance, alchemical hypnotherapy, psycho-somatic therapy, and qi gong.

Dubbed the "Dolphin Lady" by some and the "Wisdom Keeper" by others, Hannelore shares her truth through speaking, teaching and writing. In keeping with the practice of ancient and contemporary masters of unconditional love, she reveals much of what the universe has demonstrated to her through storytelling.

She has shared her messages of inspiration and divine love with audiences in Australia, Germany, Singapore, Kuala Lumpur, India, and throughout Canada and the United States. Her greatest joy is witnessing the transformation of those who read her books and/or participate in her seminars, workshops, visions quests, and retreats.

Hannelore has been deeply influenced and inspired by such renowned spiritual leaders as Ram Dass, Miguel Ruiz, Gregg Braden, Alan Cohen, Nassim Haramein, Deepak Chopra, Dr. Wayne Dyer, and the Dalai Lama.

Hannelore enjoys spending time with her two children and three grandchildren, listening to uplifting spiritual music, tending to her organic vegetable and flower gardens, and doing a variety of crafts she lovingly makes for family and friends. Her greatest passion is communing with nature as she explores remote wilderness locations.

For free gifts, to book Hannelore to speak at an event, or to register for one of her *Windows to the Soul* offerings, (including her comprehensive program the Academy for Applied Intuitive Studies), please visit her website at www.Hannelore.ca.

# Published & Forthcoming Titles

## Published Titles

**YOUR SOUL'S WHISPERS TRILOGY (First Book)**
**A Journey of Awakening** (Published June 2019)

**THE MAGIC OF ENERGY: Chakras, Auras, Crystals & Sound**
(Published November 2019)

## Forthcoming 2020 Titles

**YOUR SOUL'S WHISPERS TRILOGY (Second Book)**
**A Journey of Self-Transformation**

**DOLPHINS, WHALES & MAGICAL TALES:**
**Communing with Nature**

## Forthcoming 2021 Titles

**YOUR SOUL'S WHISPERS TRILOGY (Third Book)**
**A Journey of Essential Processes**

**PROSPERITY & MIRACLES: The Eight Laws**

**THE OTHER SIDE OF THE WINDOW:**
**Communing Beyond the Veil**

Made in the
USA
Columbia, SC

80868406R00134